©2010 by Design Media Publishing Limited
This edition published in August 2011

Design Media Publishing Limited
20/F Manulife Tower
169 Electric Rd, North Point
Hong Kong
Tel: 00852-28672587
Fax: 00852-25050411
E-mail: Kevinchoy@designmediahk.com
www.designmediahk.com

Editing: Catherine Chang
Proofreading: Qian Yin
Design/Layout: Hai Chi

ISBN 978-988-19740-3-7

Printed in China

Beauty Salons

DESIGN MEDIA PUBLISHING LIMITED

Contents

Foreword 6

Bundy Bundy 8

Granny. M 14

AVEDA Hair Salon 20

Salon Gallerie 26

Erics Paris Salon – Beijing Kerry Centre 32

Colour Bar Hairdressers 38

Hair Culture 42

La Guardia Salon 48

Han Salon de Visage 54

West Hertfordshire Hair Academy 60

Cristiano Cora Salon 64

Carmen Font Madrid Hairdresser's 70

Scissor Hands 76

Bergman Beauty Clinics MediSpa 82

Tiara 88

Haarwerk 94

Produce NARUSE	100
Imai Colore	106
4 Zoom Salon	112
Hair Salon Kasbah	118
Tierra	122
Hair Salon in Golden Hall	130
C-Style	138
Suave Hair	144
Philippe Venoux	150
Arrojo Cutler Salon	156
Hair Salon in Kolonaki	160
Produce Hashimoto	166
Cesare Ragazzi	174
Tan Bella Hair and Tanning Salon	180
Suite	186
Vasken Demirjian Salon	192
Hairstyling Nafi	198
Hairu Hair Treatment	204
Sense Spa	210
Blythe	216
Studio 1452	220
Jenny House Beauty Salon	224
kilico.	228
Hair Salon at Peter Mark College	234
Salon Salon Beaute	240
Tribeca Aoyama	246
Showhair Salon	252
Cure Salon Monsieur	258
Style Club	264
Index	270

Beauty Salons and Spatial Designs

In modern days, beauty salons are expected to be more than just a place to get a haircut.

Beauty salons used to be just a place to "become beautiful" and hairdressers' role was only to provide hairstyles that made the customers look better. Therefore, the space of a beauty salon was designed to be avant-garde and it was a place that had somewhat a sense of tension. However, nowadays, beauty salons are considered not merely as a place to "become pretty" but also as a place to "get refreshed (healed)". Many beauty salons have developed new menus such as head spa, head treatment and scalp massage to heal the customer from inside. Moreover, under the idea of "a total beauty", beauty salons also provide nail cares and eyelash extensions to cover everything concerning "beauty", and thus various functions are required in one space.

Based on this stream of beauty salons changing from a place to "become beautiful" to a place to "get refreshed (healed)", the tone of spatial designs have switched from avant-garde and tense to a warming one, using wood and plastering materials. In order to realise the idea of

"total beauty", designers use various techniques to create a space that is suitable for each function, meaning that multiple elements are combined in one space.

What I emphasise most in the midst of this change is the "philosophy" of the owners. The standard of "beauty" varies in accordance with personal tastes and it alters with time as well. However, in my point of view, the" philosophy" of the owners is universal.

I will give you examples from my past works. An owner of a beauty salon named "Tiara" said to me as below. "Tiara is a jewelry that a bride wears on her head. 'The wedding day' is the day that a woman looks most beautiful and I want to provide a service that a woman can feel as same as that special day every time she comes to my salon." In order to express the owner's "philosophy", here is what I did in the design of the salon: above each seat lies a ceiling, which you can say is a head of the space. On that ceiling, I put "islands" instead of "Tiaras" so that the customers are able to imagine about their honeymoons.

In another salon, "Produce NARUSE", the owner's "philosophy" was to make their new shop into

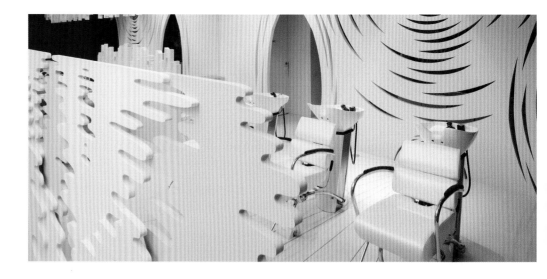

something that would link to the historical city it is located in. Every beauty salon has "partitions" to separate the space according to use (haircutting space, waiting room, reception, shampooing space and dispensary). I used the partition as well as the façade as parts of one picture. That is to say, when looking at them separately, the partitions are just regular partitions, but when looking the shop from outside, it is designed to be one big picture that would blend into the city.

I also believe that the "lighting" is the most important factor that we must consider when actually designing a space. In a beauty salon, the illuminance of a haircutting space requires to be more than 1,000 lx, which is almost equal to the colour temperature of the daytime sunlight. The illuminance for sections of nail care and eyelash extension needs to be around 700 lx to 800 lx, while make-up space requires approximately 600 lx and they use an incandescent lamp (orange light) to make the colour of the customer's face look better. Since shampooing section doesn't have to be bright at all, indirect illuminations are used to prevent the lights from getting into the customers' eyes directory and make them feel more relaxed.

By securing just enough level of illuminance in each section, the space will necessarily be divided into various atmospheres, from "tense" to "relaxing". We can create a space that is both functional and well-designed merely by changing the lights.

As stated above, beauty salons need to fulfill many conditions, but the most precious thing is the "philosophy" of the owner and there are limitless ways to respond to their needs.

Beauty salons will keep on developing, but at the same time, spatial designs will continue to advance as well.

Masahiro Yoshida
Representative Executive, KAMITOPEN Inc.

Bundy Bundy

Location:
Vienna Austria

Designer:
BWM Architekten und Partner

Photographer:
Rupert Steiner

Completion date:
2006

Bundy Bundy is the largest hairstyling firm in the high-quality segment in Austria. This internationally oriented flagship salon is a jewel in Vienna's crown. The objective is to accommodate the high art of hairstyling in a salon that cleverly combines many years of Bundy Bundy's expertise with the latest demands in the ambience and design, while featuring all elements of timeless classic.

The key focus of the concept is the customer, who will to be made to feel like guests in a five-star hotel. The concept was strongly influenced by the colour palette: each room has its own individual accent. The spectrum runs from soft light beige and strong mauve through bright magenta and lustrous mother-of-pearl all the way to relaxing mint. Sophisticated lighting design intensifies the ambience and gives each room its very own personality. Reception and lobby area with an open fireplace, bar and prominent artistic delights in a soft light brown. The lounge provides first-class treatments and indulgent experiences for the customer in a cosy atmosphere with strong mauve. The Mirror Hall is a place of transformation and an

1. The reception and lobby area are in a soft light brown
2. Large graphic pattern of bird on the wall
3. Transition area
4. Mirror-surfaced closets with set-in screens
5. The Mirror Hall is in exciting bright magenta
6. The unique-designed light fixtures

impressive backdrop for exciting new looks with bright magenta. The Crystal Hall's styling scenery like a sumptuous baroque table with a sparkling crystal waterfall and walls dipped in lustrous mother-of-pearl. The hair spa is an oasis of relaxation with washing facilities complete with massage function and soft laser applications, dominated by calming mint-green including a view of the verdant courtyard.

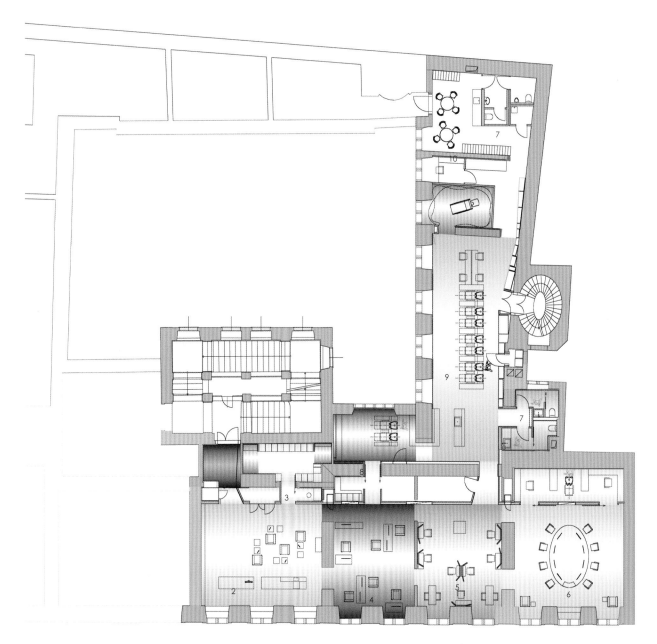

1. Entrance
2. Reception
3. Dressing room
4. Lounge
5. Mirror Hall
6. Crystal Hall
7. Toilet
8. Lounge spa
9. Hair spa
10. Waiting area

Granny. M

Location:
Toyokawa Japan

Designer:
Hiroyuki Miyake

Photographer:
Nacasa & Partners Inc.

Completion date:
2005

The designer tried to make a fictional scenery but something nostalgic, like a location of fairy-tale. Two huts were put together without thinking about where was the outside or the inside. The small one which runs through the front window is an approach from outside to inside, namely from reality to unreality. The healing/relaxing factors like shampoo, head-spa are in another hut to emphasise the interior.

The designer hopes this space tempt people to submerge themselves, because a salon should be the place for people not only to have hair cut but also to escape from their ordinary life. The requirements and the restrictions have been carefully analysed to express the space as pure as possible and make a landscape-factor in the space. The whole surface of the huts was put up of mosaic tiles with designed striped pattern, because of attempting to describe obvious space. The stripe makes directional and continual in the space. The plan was very definite, so the way of lighting was divided clearly between two huts and the other space. The illumination and the colour temperature in the huts are much lower than the outside of the huts.

1. Two huts were put together
2. The walls of the hut were put up of mosaic tiles
3. The salon provides a place for people to escape from their ordinary life, like a world of fairytale
4. The inside-out effect
5. The illumination and the colour temperature are simple

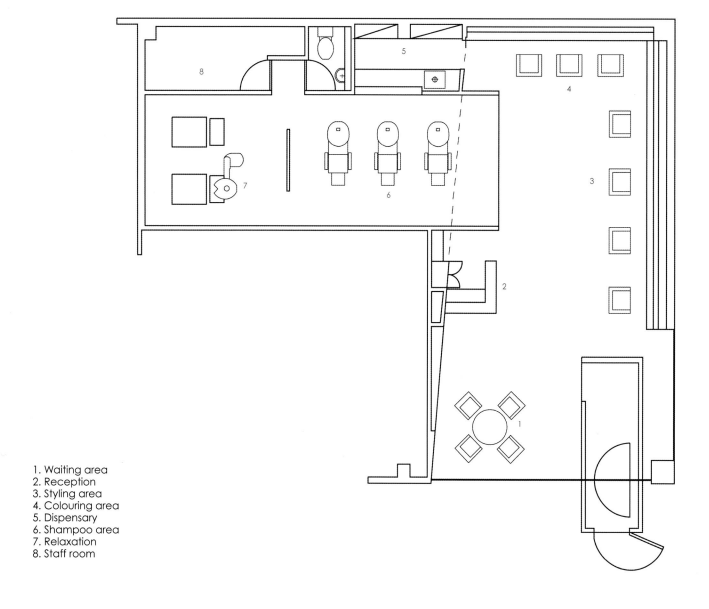

1. Waiting area
2. Reception
3. Styling area
4. Colouring area
5. Dispensary
6. Shampoo area
7. Relaxation
8. Staff room

4

AVEDA Hair Salon

Location:
Tokyo Japan

Designer:
CURIOSITY Inc.

Photographer:
CURIOSITY Inc.

Completion date:
2007

In the AVEDA Hair Salon, power and energy of nature are translated into architecture. The guests would feel like walking through a forest, surrounded by high trees. The dynamic of the space is a reminiscence of the power of nature, a series of sequences, a journey through different scene each with as specific function, a seamless space where the architecture seems suspended from above. A subtle game of transparency and reflections trigger the sensitivity and senses of the customer, to bring them closer to themselves and the essence of AVEDA.

The random of the facets is a sharp contrast with the environment, it reminds of the freedom of nature, while large wood walls structure the space into a spatial composition the reveals unexpected views and perspective as you walk through. The space seems to be created with three basic elements: water (glass), stone (concrete floor) and wood (walls). The palette of materials was kept to the minimal, the natural feel of the concrete floor, is a sharp contrast with the graphical wood structure, the light wood colour gives a fresh and natural feel gradually enlighted with linear undirect lighting.

1. The power and energy of nature
were translated into architecture
2. Terraced wood stand
3. The cutting area combines three
basic elements: water, stone and wood
4. The relaxing area is quite comfortable
5. The lighting expresses a sense of
relaxing
6. The chairs in the cutting area

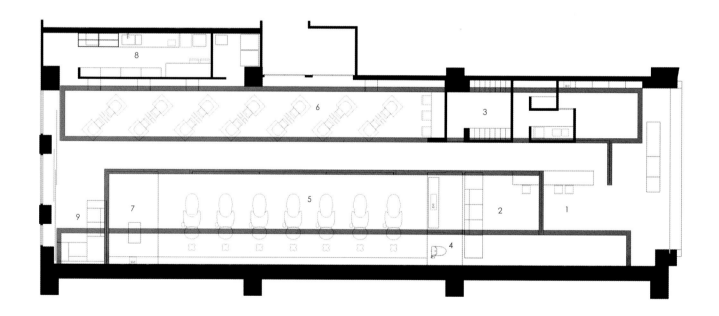

1. Reception
2. Counselling centre
3. Locker room
4. Toilet
5. Shampoo area
6. Cutting area
7. Head spa
8. Lab
9. Relaxation

Salon Gallerie

Location:
Omaha USA

Designer:
Randy Brown

Photographer:
Assassi Productions

Completion date:
2007

The project was to design a series of individual rooms to be rented out to independent entrepreneurial hair stylists. The great hair stylists are artists. They work from pictures, which clients bring in of potential hairstyles and then use their hand-eye coordination to sculpt hair into artistic compositions that complement the clients facial and body features. A great hair cut and colour transforms body and soul.

The architects decided to create the salon architecture using the hair stylist's creative process. The client gave the architects a picture of a colourful painting as the inspiration for the salon. The architects then transformed the painting into a floor plan and abruptly left the office to become the builders. Just as the hairstylist looks at a picture and then creates, sculpting as they cut, the architects began building and sculpting space based on the colourful painting. The fluid geometry of the painting was hand crafted. The transparency of the painting was sculpted from glass, perforated metal and back-lit polycarbonate. The architects took rebar and sculpted it with their hands to create sculptures for the space, abstracting hair styles and accessories. The result of this process was a space that could not have been conceived on paper. Design was created during the act of making. The architects just as the hairstylists designed with hands and eyes.

1. The project consists of a series of
individual rooms
2. An individual room viewed from
the corridor
3. Long corridor
4. Rebar sculptures
5. Interior view of an individual room

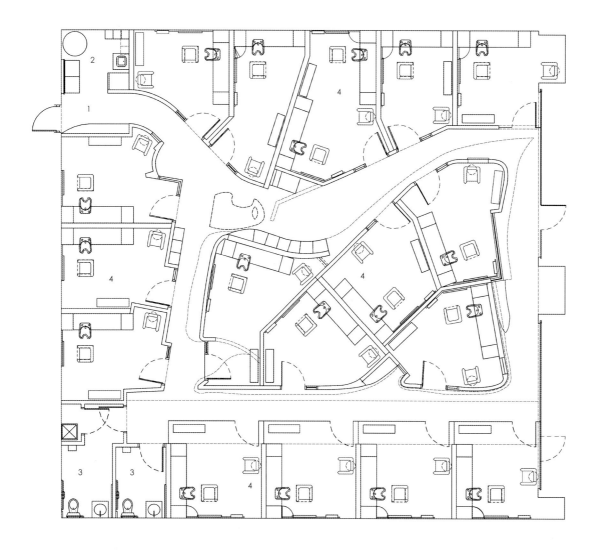

1. Entrance
2. Reception
3. Toilet
4. Individual styling rooms

1

ERIC Paris Salon – Beijing Kerry Centre

Location:
Beijing China

Designer:
GRAFT

Photographer:
Yang Di

Completion date:
2008

The remodel of ERIC Paris Salon started with the need for a connection between the newly acquired second floor space, which will house the hair cutting stations in the future, to the existing salon entrance, retail space and reception located on the ground floor.

GRAFT introduced a continuous fluid staircase, linking these two spaces together and creating a vertical "cat walk". This main vertical circulation becomes the central spine which branches off and connects the different functional areas throughout the salon. As the stair ascends, it morphs from staircase, to wall panel, until it loops over to become a fully enclosed corridor before it spills out onto the second floor. The sculptural stair is accentuated on the inside by cladding of colourful metal panels, mimicking the salons shiny and sensuous, bold, fingernail colours, while the polished stainless steel on the outside will provide customers with distorted reflections of themselves after their beauty treatment. The manicure and pedicure stations are set off as galleries for clients to admire the other roaming customers; hidden beauty rooms contain custom-designed massage tables and leather wall patterns.

1. Brightly lighted display area
2. Main cutting area was arranged
around a large table
3. The hidden beauty room contains
leather wall patterns
4. Overlooking the reception and
entrance from the fluid staircase
5. The separate styling room provides
full-services to VIP guests
6. The manicure stations
7. The waiting area and corridor

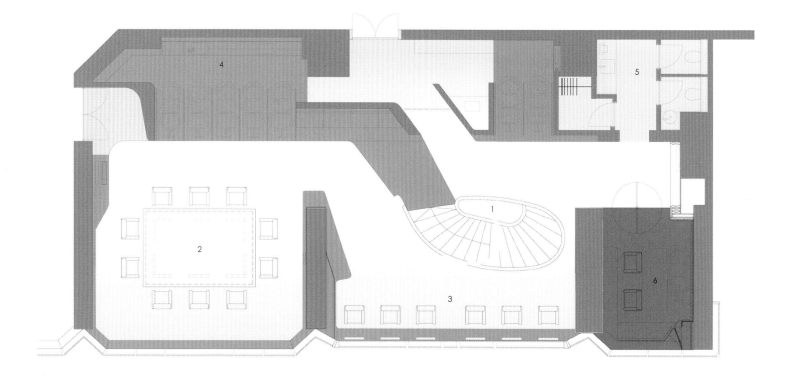

1. Staircase
2. Cutting area
3. Manicure stations
4. Shampoo area
5. Toilet
6. Separate styling room

Colour Bar Hairdressers

Location:
Prospect Australia

Designer:
Studio Nine

Photographer:
Sarah Long Photography

Completion date:
2007

Colour Bar Hairdressers was to engage the idea of the shop as a "place" rather than a traditional "shop". This shop is a unique "Colour Bar" experience but not just a "hair cut". This was achieved by creating a colourful and dynamic space, which was filled with light, sound, the aroma of coffee, colour, cutting, style and service. The shop invents a new and exciting retail image and store concept for the emerging Colour Bar hair dressing chain. The fitout was derived from a carefully formulated "Kit of Parts" that was unique to the Colour Bar Salon. This design strategy has been followed through in two later Colour Bar Stores. They all form distinctive "working zones" with a memorable "Retail Image" for the chain.

These unique devices include the idea of a coffee bar as a waiting area and attracting passing by clientele; the integration of a colour lab as an internal working feature and an area of interaction; the use of music and visual elements with colourful dynamic bulkheads and innovative lighting. Other shop parts include a Colour Waiting Area, feature Cutting Stations, window waiting bench seating, Nails table amongst others.

1. General view of the storefront
2. The reception with tall stolls
3. The red lanterns will catch passers-by's eyes
4. The cutting area and shampoo area were combined together

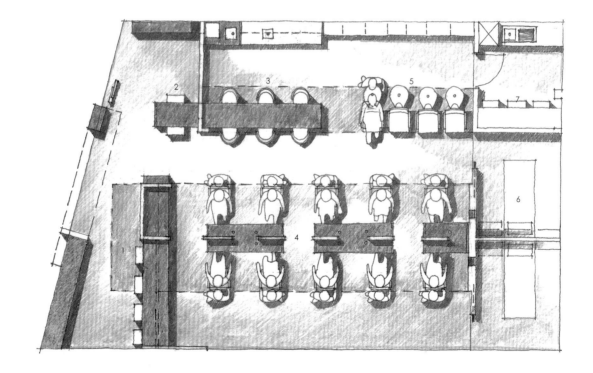

1. Reception
2. Manicure station
3. Waiting area
4. Cutting area
5. Shampoo area
6. Beauty rooms
7. Staff kitchen

Hair Culture

Location:
Taipei China

Designer:
CJ STUDIO

Photographer:
Marc Gerritsen

Completion date:
2007

Situated in the alley lane, Hair Culture is a salon which has combined with fashion elements to provide individual expert hair care and design. Using the dark brown laser-perforated metallic net to engrave the pattern of waves, it was created to bring a variety of layers and shading effects within the space. At the same time, it is a metaphor of foams and bubbles, which formed during hair washing, and emphasis the figure of water. As such, a façade of a glowing black diamond being surrounded by metallic foams can somewhat be seen from far.

The premises were divided into two floors. The core space for both the first and second floor was the mineral modules which were sculpted by black mirror glasses. Hiding behind the mineral modules, there are VIP rooms and other functional sections such as the washing area, the staff room and etc. Within the white painted space, the multilateral geometrical cut was employed on the ceilings, with the addition of brown epoxy floor, reinforcing the image of natural mineral rocks. Besides, chairs and sofas placed in the cutting and waiting area are all designed by CJ Studio. The warm grey leather of the chairs cleverly complements the white wall and the brown floor, preventing the atmosphere being overly stiff.

1. The custom-designed chair is aesthetic and comfortable
2. A façade of a glowing black diamond
3. The shampoo area uses indirect lighting
4. The lighting in cutting area and shampoo area contrast each other
5. VIP room is private
6. The perforated metallic brings a variety of layers and shading effects within the space
7. Viewing the salon through coloured glass in the staircase

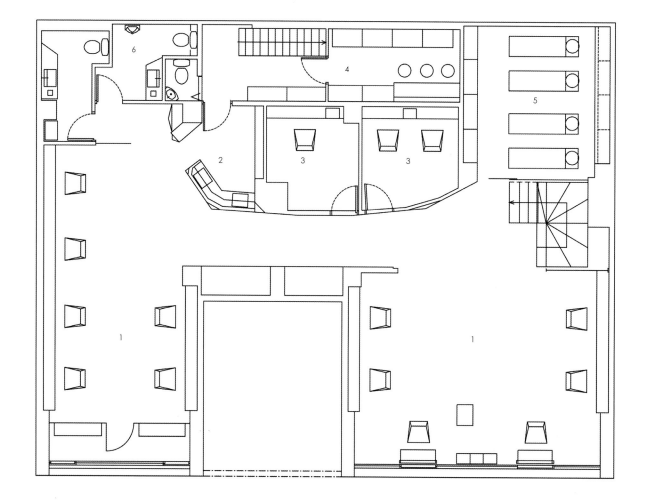

1. Cutting area
2. Colour bar
3. VIP room
4. Staff room
5. Shampoo area
6. Toilet

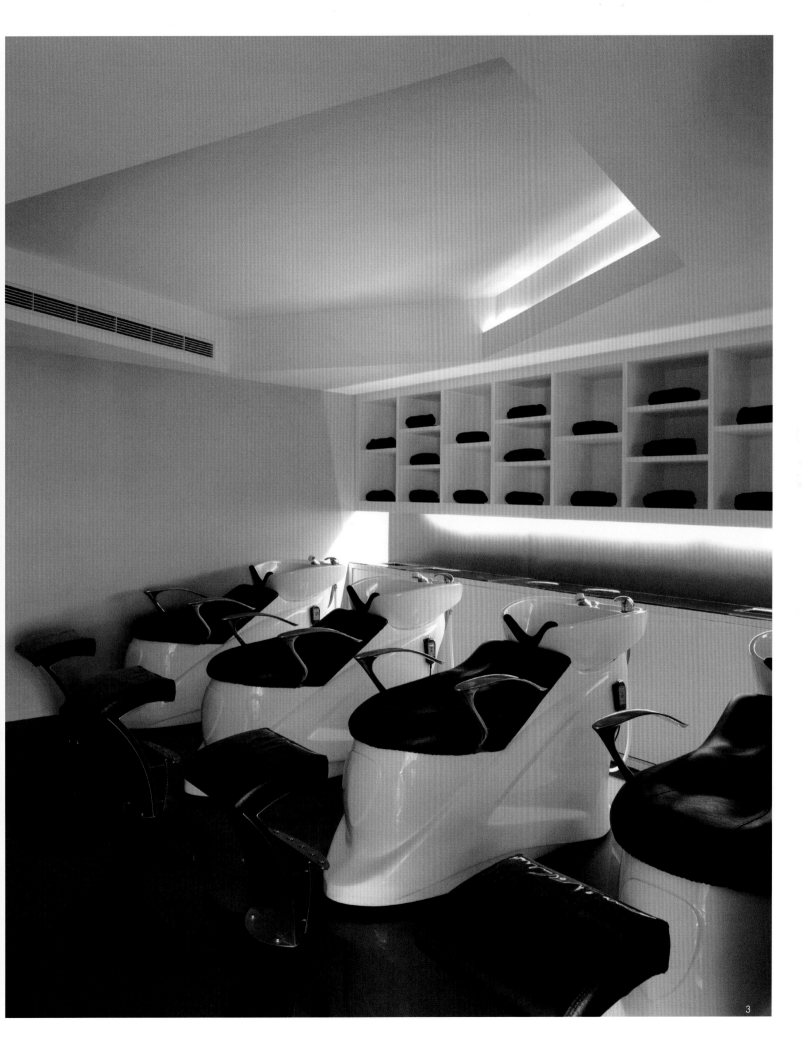

4

5

La Guardia Salon

Location:
West Village USA

Designer:
Z-A and Cheng+Snyder

Photographer:
Danny Bright

Completion date:
2007

Heightening the experience of sensory attentiveness provided the conceptual basis for the design. All of the major salon components doubly function as programme and frame. These frames, outlined in red, draw your attention to specific views, whether it is the sight of yourself in a mirror or of the receptionist through the frame of the reception desk. The waiting area, cutting stations, storage units, colour bar, espresso bar and lounge are likewise all defined in a series of frames. The adjacencies and overlaps between the frames animate the space.

On the one side the exposed brick wall was treated as a found object, where all the items that run along the wall are seen as graphic elements. The pipes and electric conduits are exposed lines that fit the red outlined frames between them. On the other side of the salon, white sheetrock wall was treated as a pliable material where the wall itself was bent and stretched, and the red frames were carved into the wall. Extending the sheetrock wall to merge with the ceiling and the brick wall to merge with the floor created an atypical configuration of the surfaces. The lighting

1. The frames create layered effect
2. The red frames with mirrors will contain customers, images
3. A separate cutting station in the corner
4. View from the entrance
5. The frames of different sizes
6. The reception and display area
7. The whole space has a red tone

scheme of vertical fluorescent lights, serve as an additional graphic system that outlines the individual spaces within the red frames. On the brick wall the fluorescents were surface mounted to highlight the texture of the wall. On the sheetrock wall lights were located within the carved frames to wash the white walls with the reflected red light.

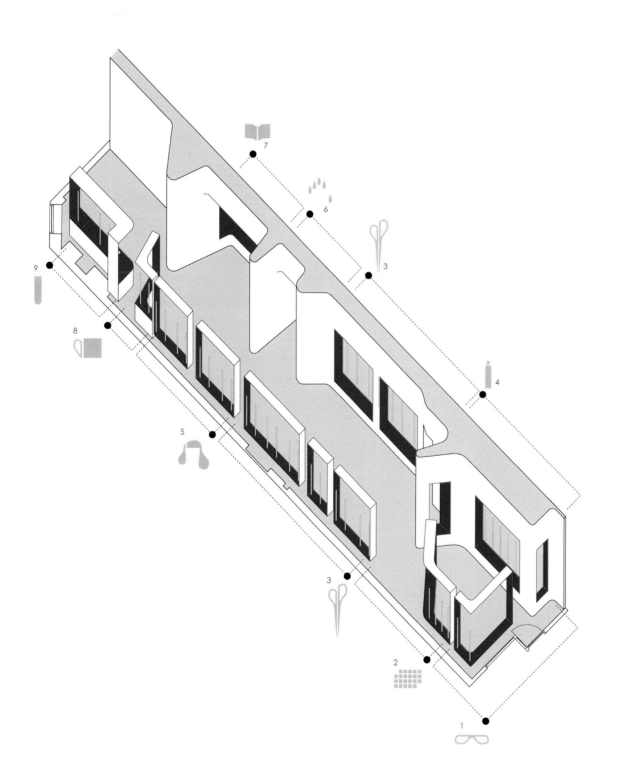

1. Entrance
2. Reception
3. Cutting area
4. Colouring area
5. Styling area
6. Shampoo area
7. Staff room
8. Waiting area
9. Lab

Han Salon de Visage

Location:
Tokyo Japan

Designer:
ICHIRO NISHIWAKI

Completion date:
2007

Han Salon de Visage is on the third floor of a building located at a residential district in Aoyama, Tokyo, which is very famous for many brand shops. This esthetic salon is a franchise shop of famous esthetician in Korea. Treatment using many kinds of potent stone is this shop's character. The designers remove the sentiments of the general public from entrance space and create a luxury space. Conductor to private room is sharp, so it reminds customers of guest rooms in a luxury hotel. Regarding the waiting room, the designers construct tenderness and high quality space with combination of gorgeous touch of carpet and fringe curtain.

1. Indirect lighting creates an intimate space
2. The salon is a place full of luxury
3. The purple velvet sheet shines slightly in the obscure lighting
4. A luxurious crystal chandelier in the corridor
5. White beam-screen in the corridor

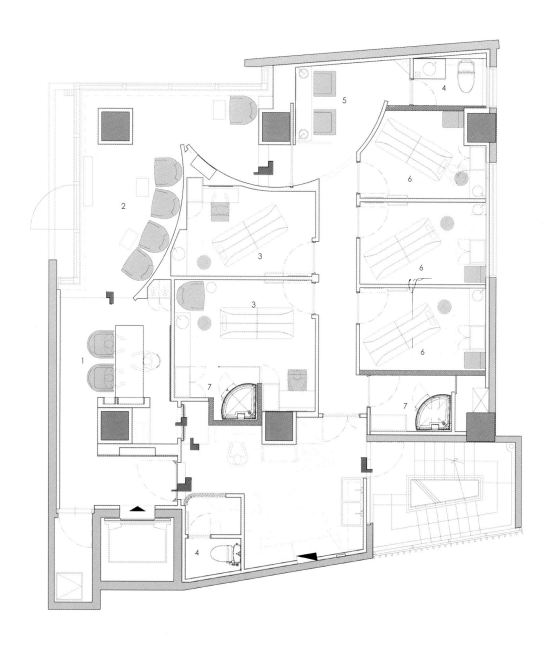

1. Reception
2. Waiting area
3. VIP treatment room
4. Toilet
5. Make-up corner
6. Treatment room
7. Shower booth

West Hertfordshire Hair Academy

Location:
Hertfordshire UK

Designer:
Tony Kerby and John Carrabin

Completion date:
2005

The designers were commissioned to convert an existing storage area into a state-of-the-art hair academy at West Hertfordshire College of Further Education. This re-branding of the facility on a more prominent part of the campus created a "real world" salon environment for the students, whilst being more friendly for them, staff and visitors. The design was organised around a reception hub area, with students progressing through the space to the final "aspiration area". The atmosphere of the academy is contemporary but with softer tones of colour, wooden flooring and better quality lighting.

1. View from the street
2. Chairs arranged in a line
3. The circle reception with circle ceiling
4. The black chairs are highlighted in
a white background

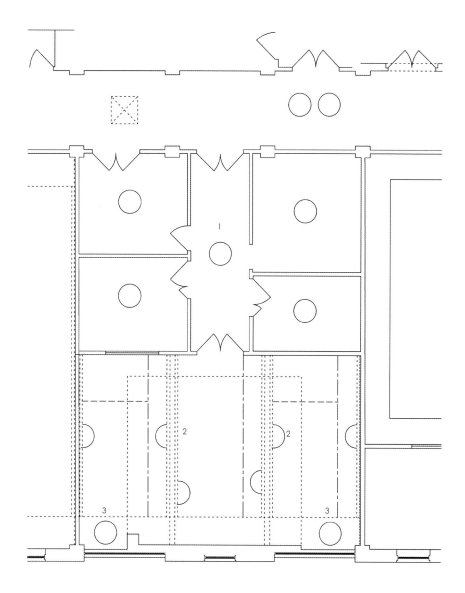

1. Reception
2. Styling area
3. Shampoo area

1

Cristiano Cora Salon

Location:
New York City USA

Designer:
Avi Oster Studio

Completion date:
2008

The goal was to create a new essence of salon environment that captures the balance between modern architecture and the needs of the hair dressing industry. The fluid movement of the Cristiano Cora Salon truly captures the elements of simple modern design while the functionality of the design enables a smoother process of hair dressing.

The vision for this project evolved gradually. The designer's aim was to create a space that would be distinctly appealing to women; something slightly curved, clean and stylish, but at the same time comforting and being transformational. The designer tried to keep everything clean and to eliminate as much information or distraction besides the experience of the client and the stylist. For instance, there is a separate wet and dry room for laundry services which is kept discreet by a hidden door. The designer also designed the floor to curve upwards to enable easy sweeping of the hair to the vacuum system's nozzles at the edge of the floor.

The experience of the client is one of transformation. At Cristiano, the simplicity of the design encourages the client's focus to be on the inspiring experience of becoming transformed. In this salon, the designer wanted to create the sensation for a woman to enter a protected space and emerge transformed; they would feel purified, indulged, comforted and relaxed.

1. It is a space of pure white
2. High-fashion chairs in the waiting area
3. The red shampoo chairs add colour
to the white space
4. View from the entrance
5. The reception is merged in the floor
and wall
6. View from the inner part of the salon

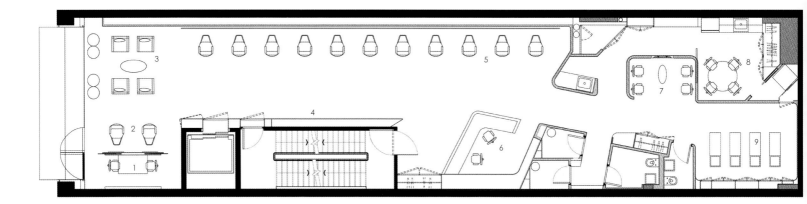

1. Office
2. Styling room 1
3. Waiting area
4. Display area
5. Styling room 2
6. Reception
7. Dry room
8. Staff room
9. Shampoo area

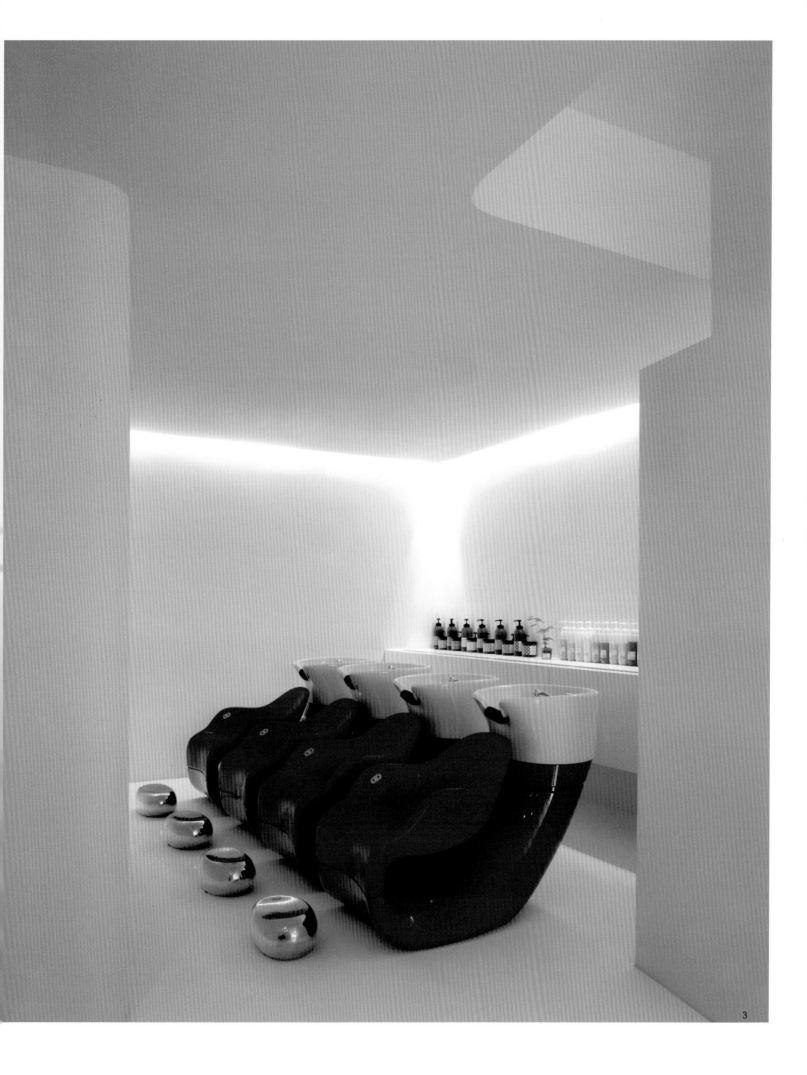

4

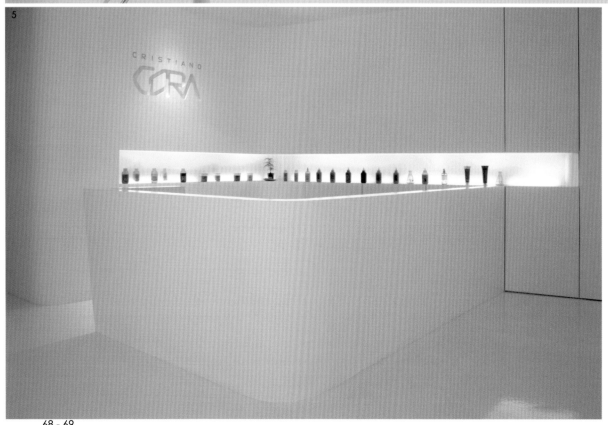

5

Carmen Font Madrid Hairdresser's

Location:
Madrid Spain

Designer:
Diego & Pedro Serrano (innova::
designers studio)

Completion date:
2008

The own charm of the space, located in the historical zone of the opera, in Madrid, made us to be respectful. That's why the designers get the hairdresser's ready to have an unforgettable night at the opera: the interior design is reminiscent of a sophisticated and avant-garde suit or dress, black for men and with transparents clothes for women (the walls and the mirrors). The designers also made a previous hair implant on the walls, which resembles the glamous hairstyle appropriated to the circumstances. In this hairdresser's, there is glamour and glamour.

1. The storefront has a retro look
2. The interior lighting creates a glamorous effect
3. The waiting area is extremely ancient with its stone walls
4. Black walls with hair implant
5. The transparent glass mirror frame
6. The entrance and waiting area

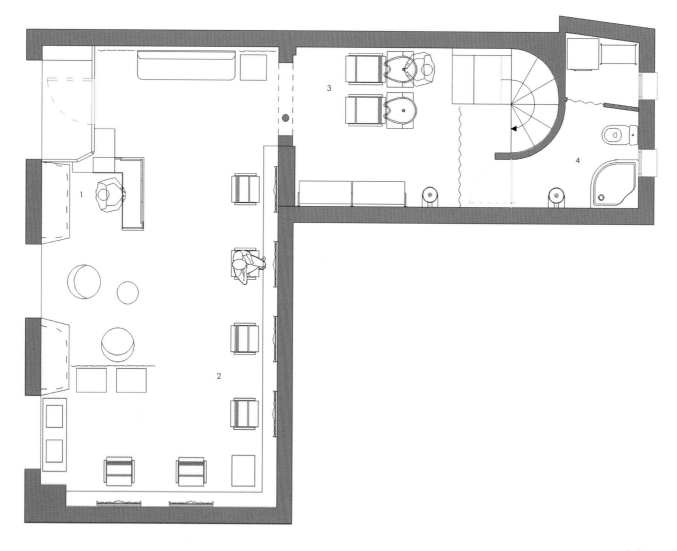

1. Reception
2. Cutting area
3. Shampoo area
4. Toilet

Scissor Hands

Location:
Istanbul Turkey

Designer:
Nagehan Acimuz

Completion date:
2006

Scissor Hands was designed as a dynamic and energetic hairdresser that offers women and men hairstyles together. The space already had a warm effect and had all the right conditions to turn itself into a cosy home like atmosphere. The hairdresser was divided into three sections. The ground floor space was designed for men, the first floor was designed for women and the basement section used for serving and office spaces.

At the linear and horizontal surfaces, mosaic, natural stone, timber, glass and certainly the mirrors and their relations with each other had been used in a balanced way. The designers have selected special motifs, pictures and words and used them as sticker on the walls that turns some parts of the space into a romantic atmosphere.

As the owner did not want the inside to be seen much, the designers have created a façade that would satisfy their needs, at the same time, designed huge glass walls in the entrance part, so that the huge motif on the wall can be seen from outside giving clues about the function of the space. Outside becomes in, inside becomes out. Lighting armatures and lighting levels were very important because of the function of the space, and soft lighting combines with natural materials to create a warm, welcoming feel.

1. Wood floor in cutting area creates a relaxing atmosphere
2. There is a pair of large eyes on the wall behind the reception
3. Waiting room is provided with TV and coffee bar
4. The lighting in cutting area is warm and soft
5. Overall view of the lower floor salon
6. Shampoo chairs are very comfortable
7. Along staircase, there are fashion wallpapers

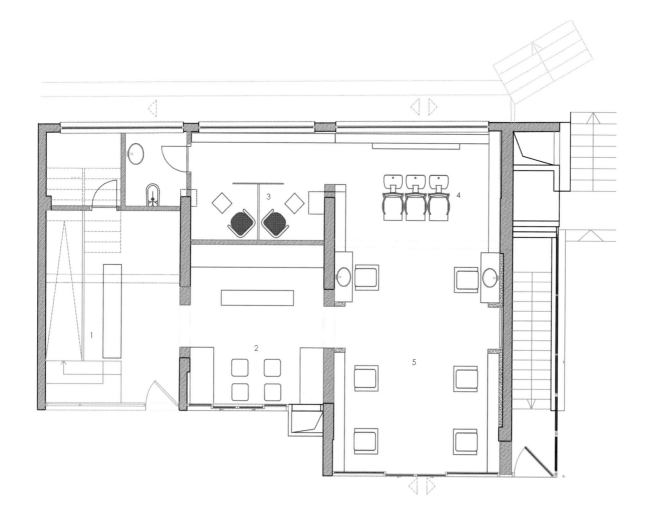

1. Reception
2. Waiting room
3. VIP styling room
4. Shampoo area
5. Styling area

4

5

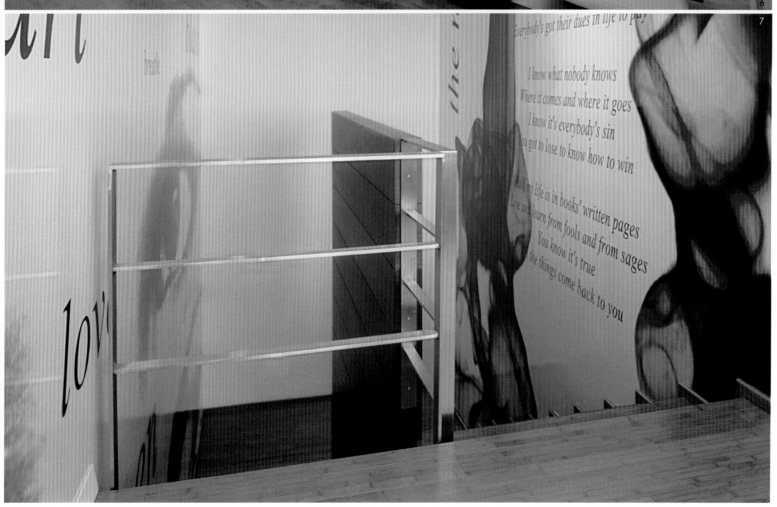

Everybody's got their dues in life to pay

I know what nobody knows
Where it comes and where it goes
I know it's everybody's sin
You got to lose to know how to win

Half my life is in books' written pages
Live and learn from fools and from sages
You know it's true
the things come back to you

Bergman Beauty Clinics MediSpa

Location:
Amsterdam The Netherlands

Designer:
Concrete Architectural Associates

Completion date:
2008

Bergman is all about beauty. The best item to express beauty is a mirror and therefore this is the cental theme of the MediSpa. These mirrors are used in the three areas of the MediSpa: the shop, the treatment rooms and the main surgery room. It enlarges the rooms and creates a spacious feeling.

When clients enter the MediSpa they are invited to take a seat in the heart of the shop: an island made of corian and smooth white leather surrounded by Bergman's beauty products and magazines. Floating white corian cabinets, filled with and coloured by Bergman's beauty products give costumers the opportunity to try the products such as crèmes and make-up. Inside the four treatment rooms, located on both floors, a spacious and cosy environment is waiting for their clients. Full-length mirrors create the impression of an even more spacious room. White corian cabinets and semi-transparent curtains give the room a smooth and clean appearance. In the surgery room consumers encounter an open atmosphere. Cabinets of stainless steel, filled with bottles of alcohol give visitors the suggestion of being in a laboratory. A big surgical light is hanging above the white treatment chair.

1. A mirror wall with the brand's logo enlarges the whole space
2. The treatment room has a spacious and cosy environment
3. Customers can either read magazines or watch TV in the waiting area
4. The main surgery room
5. An island made of corian and smooth white leather surrounded by Bergman's beauty products and magazines
6. The doctor's office was combined with the surgery room

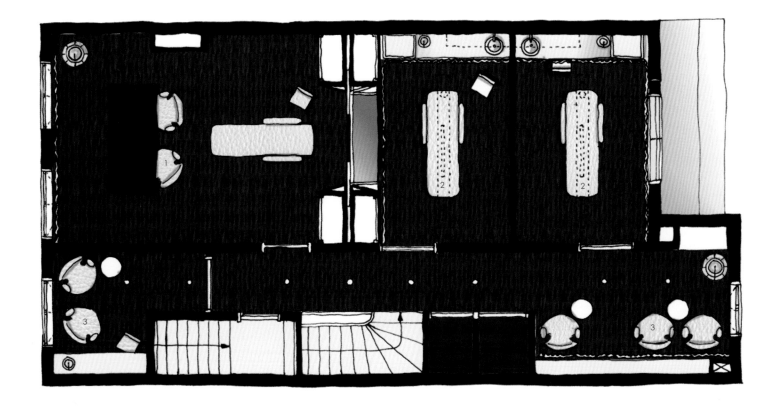

1. Main surgery room
2. Treatment room
3. Waiting area

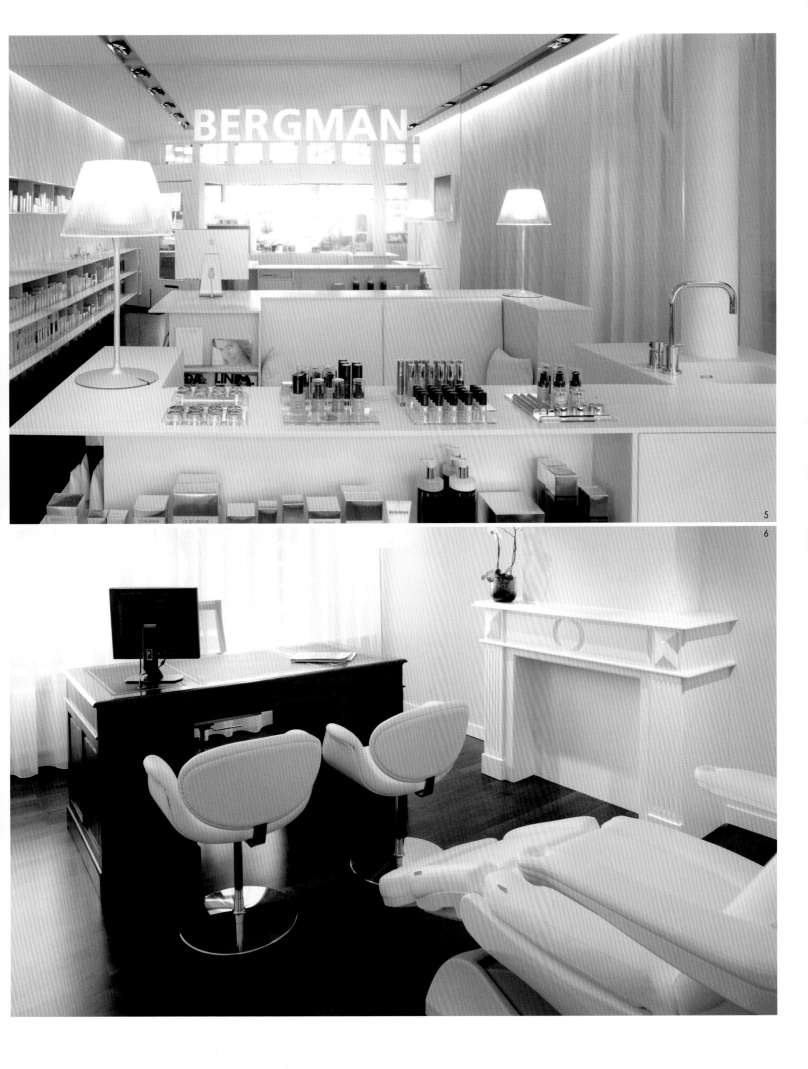

Tiara

Location:
Sendai Japan

Designer:
KAMITOPEN Inc./Masahiro Yoshida

Photographer:
Keisuke Miyamoto

Completion date:
2009

Tiara is a motif of accessories that brides wear. The hair salon's concept is "wedding day and the women's beautiful moment". The hair salon is located at a retail area in Aoba-ku, Sendai. The interior design represents high quality for the high end customers and shows the owner's high fashion concepts.

People consciously make barriers to the outside and make their own territory at anytime and anyplace. Therefore, the designer designed floating island ceiling, which was changed by reflecting chairs' shape to make customers feel vague and invisible barriers at this salon. Each island floats in the air like customers' own island. Those islands can help people sitting on the chair recognise their own place.

Practically, this island works as board reflector, all light falling onto the floor from this island. In addition, this falling light was specially designed. The light, which is falling onto the pathway from entrance to setting place, is soft amber light in order to represent "sunset". The light, which falling onto the setting area, is white flesh light in order to represent "sunrise". In result, those lights create rainbows at shampoo booth through illuminating double-layered ceilings at shampoo booth and create prismatic effect through triangle glass pole that was placed at shampoo booth entrance.

1. The VIP room has brown and white leather wall, showing a sense of luxury
2. Above each seat floats an island
3. The reception
4. Comfortable shampoo beds
5. The make-up room looks like a wonderland
6. The corridor to the main salon

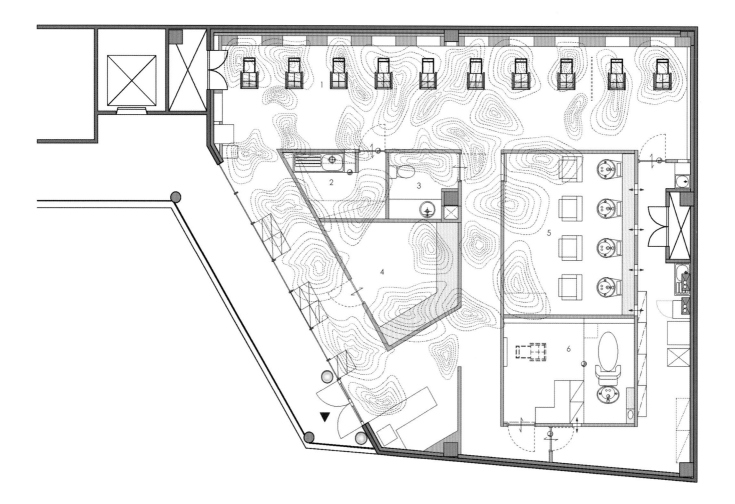

1. Cutting area
2. Lab
3. Toilet
4. Make-up room
5. Shampoo room
6. VIP styling room

Haarwerk

Location:
Cologne Germany

Designer:
Hackenbroich Architekten

Photographer:
Hackenbroich Architekten

Completion date:
2008

For the hairdresser shop Haarwerk in Cologne, Germany the light installation has become a main spatial feature. Seventy-five lamps emerge from a central point of the space and reach out into the room. A cloud of lights expands through the store. With the visible wires they form a spatial texture like a distorted chandelier. The lights can be controlled and dimmed in five circles to allow a smooth transition of various illuminated conditions.

The overall organisation of the store was challenged by the spatial limitation of the old factory building. To maintain a coherent spatial experience while accommodating all functional areas, the designers decided to "extrude" the enclosed functional areas from the back-wall. The surface of the wall "remained" on the volumes/furniture while the other surfaces "merged" with the floor.

The materials fluctuate between a refined and rough appearance. While the wallpaper has a subtle elegance the lamps have an industrial quality. The colours articulate the volumetric logic by continuing the dark grey of the floor or the ginger marking the sidewalls of the store. The lights, when partially dimmed, combine the white of the wallpaper, the ginger of the wall and the dark grey of the floor.

1. General view from the entrance
2. The light installation has become a main spatial feature
3. The white of the wallpaper, the ginger of the wall and the dark grey of the floor are combined together
4. All the cabinets are either white or dark grey
5. The space with natural light
6. The wallpaper has a subtle elegance

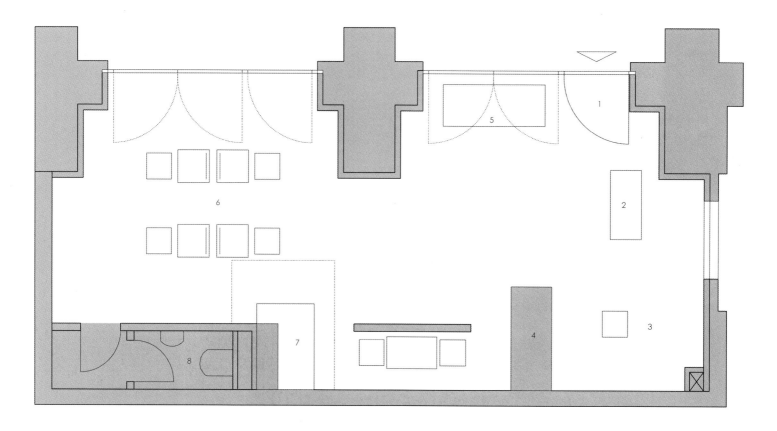

1. Entrance
2. Reception
3. Shampoo area
4. Wardrobe/storage
5. Waiting area
6. Work places
7. Kitchen
8. Toilet

Produce NARUSE

Location:
Machida Japan

Designer:
KAMITOPEN Inc./Masahiro Yoshida

Photographer:
Keisuke Miyamoto

Completion date:
2008

Located in residential streets, this salon opens on road, and it has more than tripled depth than openings width. The concept of this project is "Sense of Vision" to enhance to keep the relationship between outside and inside and impact each other by using necessary elements for salons.

Today, the method of divideing individual spaces by partition is frequently used in order to keep customers' privacy, especially in this kind of retail shops. This method can make individual spaces rich and special. Moreover, the technique can spoil fascination as total space. This salon consists of five partitions: Outside Wall, which is dividing outside and inside; Partition 2, which is dividing waiting area and cut area; Partition 3, which is dividing cut area and shampoo area; Partition 4, which is dividing shampoo area and exclusive cut area; Partition 5, which is dividing shampoo area and space for colour dispensers. Those five partitions are normal partitions when customers see one by one. The partitions can be turned to one picture when customers look at distance.

1. Partitions divide individual spaces, and that is the main feature
2. The exclusive cutting area uses crack-style indirect lighting in the ceiling
3. The lighting in shampoo area is dimmed
4. The pure white shampoo area
5. The main cutting area
6. Viewing from the street, the partitions turn to one picture

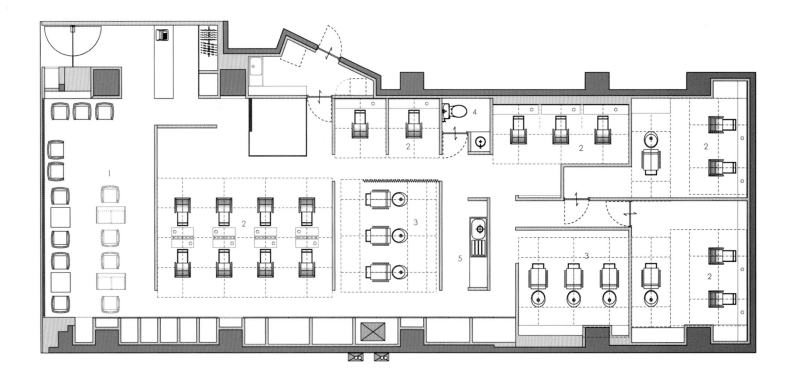

1. Inner styling room
2. Styling area
3. Shampoo area
4. Toilet
5. Lab

Imai Colore

Location:
Tokyo Japan

Designer:
Edward Suzuki

Photographer:
Yasuhiro Nukamura

Completion date:
2007

This beauty parlor is located in the basement of the newly completed "Omote-Sando Hills" complex in posh Harajuku district of Tokyo. "Imai Colore" is a "total beauty salon" boasting 424 square metres of floor space and is one of the largest shops in the new commercial complex. It features basically hair colouring (Colore), facial and body care (Suite), and a flower shop (Odette) by the entrance.

"Relaxation" was the key design concept. To achieve this objective a gently falling waterfall of three metres tall, twenty metres long with a pool of reflective water was planned as a highlighting feature. The water "wall" consists of corrugated glass backlit to provide a warm, indirect lighting effect. Customers can sit in front of the pool to enjoy the beauty and the serenity of the atmosphere, watching and/or listening to the sound of the gentle waterfall. Mirrors of polished stainless steel were erected as free-standing plates that almost disappear in the man-made landscape.

Lighting was deliberately kept minimal only to shine on the customers' faces and heads as well as to highlight certain attractions such as the water and the green planted in and out of the pool. Attracted into the shop by the scent of flowers by the entrance, customers once inside cannot help but sense a feeling of being in a Zen garden of tranquility, serenity and harmony, only to come out totally relaxed and refreshed.

1. The sweet smell of flowers makes a sense of relaxation
2. Customers will face the pool while enjoying hairdressing services
3. The face & body treatment room
4. The shampoo area
5. The round reception is back-lit
6. The water wall provides a warm, indirect lighting effect

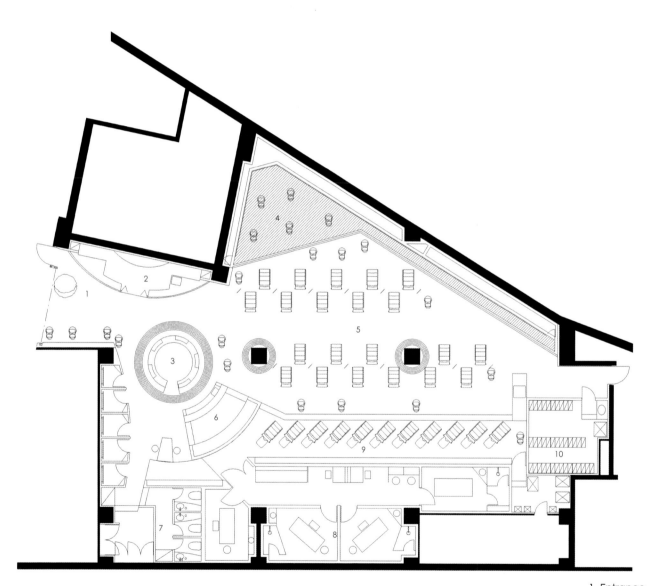

1. Entrance
2. Flower shop
3. Reception
4. Pond
5. Colour and blow area
6. Waiting area
7. Toilet
8. Face & body treatment
9. Shampoo area
10. Staff room

4 Zoom Salon

Location:
Taipei China

Designer:
M. Design/Stephen Kuo

Photographer:
Kyle Yu

Completion date:
2008

Vision and circulation guide trend of space. Independent ladder is used with pure white ceiling and terrace, echoing with modern keynote. White terrace at the entrance was integrated in space. Main visual axis with L-shape framework collocating with shape wraparound demarcation, exposing architecture body and dragging out of infinite tension of space.

At the entrance, bar counter which is like wooden box sets off the wood grain ceiling and terrace more naturally through leaning narrow angle and oblique angle, which gives prominence to unique charm of dark black beam column. Dying and perming area keeps the rounded hollow-out, which is near the window, and it is the best position for viewing landscape. Natural light is brought into interior space, which makes this area integrate with outdoor green colour, so as to make people enjoy joyful and comfortable atmosphere.

Behind bar counter, there is a haircutting area organised by some wooden boxes. At the end part, bar code style mirror faces with unsymmetrical cuttings enfold and stand side by side, which reflect corresponding relationship of spatial texture and create an order.

1. General view of the salon
2. The reception is designed like a bar
3. Customers can have an outdoor view through the mirror
4. The rounded windows provide natural light for the interior
5. The bar's leaning narrow angle gives prominence to unique charm of dark black beam column
6. The cutting area consists of wooden shelves
7. At the end of the salon is bar code style mirror faces with unsymmetrical cuttings

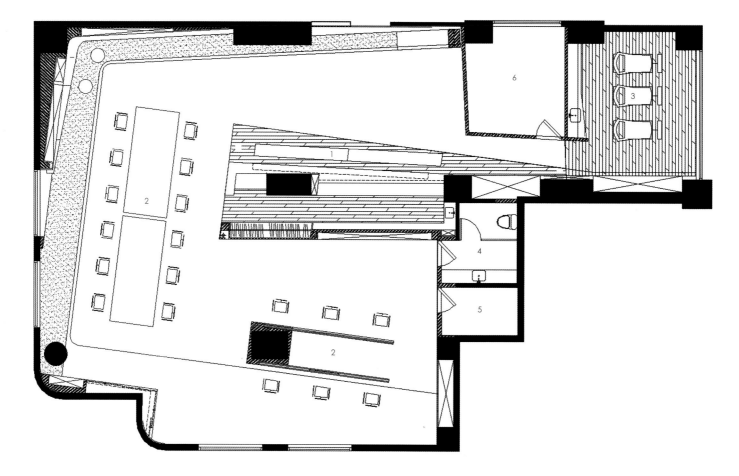

1. Reception
2. Styling area
3. Shampoo room
4. Toilet
5. SPA room
6. Staff room

Hair Salon Kasbah

Location:
Nagano Japan

Designer:
no.555 – Tsuchida Takuya

Photographer:
Torimura Koichi

Completion date:
2007

The site is located in a business district where unplaned land lines up in the heartland of Nagano Prefecture. The house with the hair salon was planned here. First of all, walls were planned around the site to guard the site from the neighbourings. The functional area is inserted deeply in the second and the third floor to secure the lighting and ventilation.

The hair salon is located on the first floor. Since the salon is targeted to the middle-age, the building looks sealed to give the brand image of "the customer is covered and secured". The building is designed to secure residential comfort and salon brand at same time to endure the surrounding change in the future.

1. The salon is an open space
2. There's a void between the envelope and the window wall
3. General view of the salon
4. The French windows provide natural light

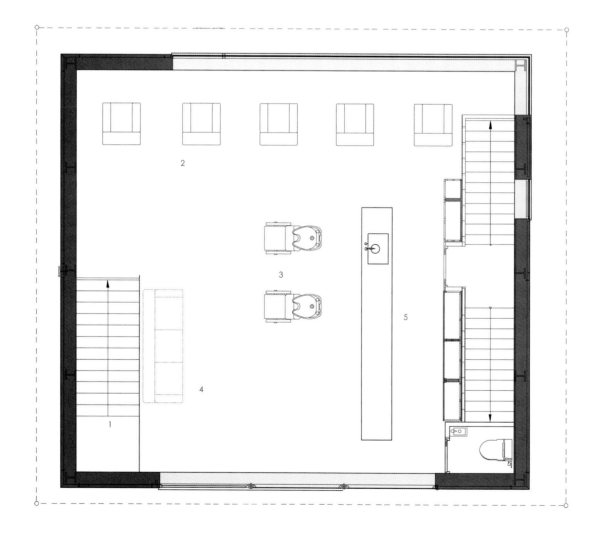

1. Staircase
2. Cutting area
3. Shampoo area
4. Waiting area
5. Lab

3

4

Tierra

Location:
Tokyo Japan

Designer:
Ryo Matsui Architects

Photographer:
T. Hiraga

Completion date:
2008

This hair salon is located in the Tokyo city centre. It is a salon which consists of haircut area, shampoo area, head-spa room, arrangement area and VIP rooms to treat people's hair comprehensively. The client wanted the space with tranquility and spirituality in a restricted basement level.

A large number of mirrors, whose quantities unfamiliar in an ordinary architectural space, are indispensable inside the salon. Focusing on this particular condition and treating the "mirror" as one of the major component in the space formulation, the designers have attempted to deal with the function as a material instead of the space being dominated by the function. Moreover, this notion will ensure users the dramatic experience of space, including the transition of space from outside, by perceiving this context positively. Mirror's original intention of reflecting people has disappeared, and it has become an architectural portion to reflect the space itself. People will see themselves reflected in the space and will be able to reflect on oneself instead of just seeing oneself reflected in the mirror.

1. The arches remind people of an European palace
2. The space has a warm colour tone
3. In head spa room, the lighting in the ceiling looks like stars
4. The open space has a generous and relaxing effect
5. The reception
6. The lighting design is both aesthetic and functional
7. The entrance to the salon
8. Mirrors have a magical effect in the salon design

The designers have also done trial calculations on lighting to allocate both appropriate quality and quantity of lighting equipment, not only from the aesthetician's functional point of view, but for the user's comfort in this space. The material covering the wall and ceiling was finished by the craftsman with the special coating containing soil and aggregate. Delicate uneven texture that contradicts with the mirror accentuates the silhouette of the arch.

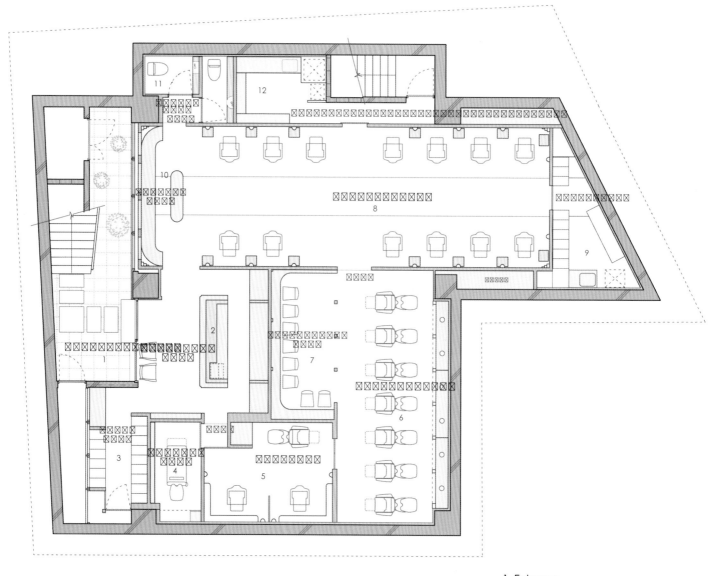

1. Entrance
2. Reception
3. Cloak room
4. Head SPA room
5. VIP room
6. Shampoo area
7. Arrangement area
8. Cutting area
9. Staff room
10. Waiting area
11. Toilet
12. Preparation room for hair arrangement

5

6

Hair Salon in Golden Hall

Location:
Athens Greece

Designer:
Gfra Architecture

Photographer:
Fotis Traganoudakis

Completion date:
2009

The hair salon is situated in the Golden Hall Shopping Centre in Marousi, Athens, next to the Olympic Stadium. The space was divided vertically into two areas. On the ground floor the welcome and service desk is located parallel to the linearly positioned hair-dressing tables. The mezzanine is used for more private functions such as manicure, pedicure and the massage area.

The overall space is designed combining two elements: the existing shell, with an industrial character, referring to the construction phase, and the new shell, using free forms and more refined materials to address the function of the shop. Therefore, the materials and colours chosen to support this concept are concrete-like cement plaster on the walls, industrial cement flooring and visible metal structures for the new walls made of gypsum board and unpainted sheet metal for the service and bar desk. The minimal stair, with triangular visible metal steps leads to the metal mezzanine construction. The floor of the mezzanine is also covered with untreated metal sheets.

The rough industrial character of these materials is contrasted by a choice of more refined materials suitable for a hairdressing environment. Thus parts of the walls and ceilings were covered with vinyl wallpaper; the hair-dressing desks and the sinks were shaped out of Corian, and completed with a wide use of mirrors, both for functional and decorative reason.

1. The hair-dressing tables were arranged in a line
2. The space has an industrial atmosphere
3. The reception parallels with the hair-dressing tables
4. Black and white contrast each other
5. The mezzanine is used for manicure, pedicure and the massage area
6. The floor of the mezzanine is covered with untreated metal sheets
7. The washing room
8. View from the entrance
9. View from the back of the mezzanine
10. Comfortable and simple-designed shampoo chairs

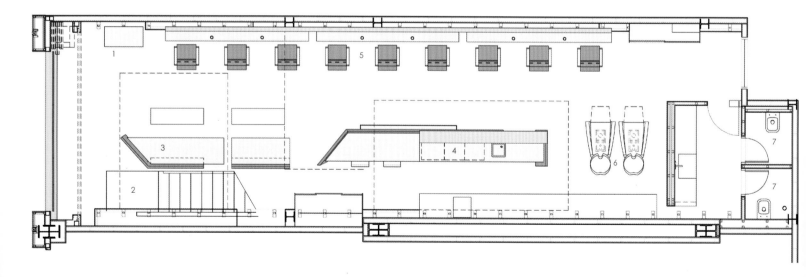

1. Entrance
2. Stair to mezzanine
3. Waiting area
4. Reception
5. Cutting area
6. Shampoo area
7. Toilet

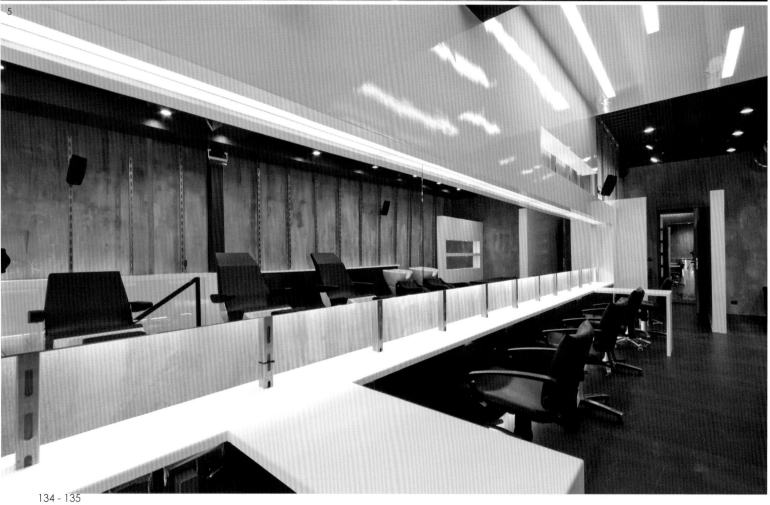

C-Style

Location:
Saitama Japan

Designer:
KAMITOPEN Inc./Masahiro Yoshida

Photographer:
Keisuke Miyamoto

Completion date:
2009

The C-Style Salon's concepts are "Clean, Care and Colour" and its hair colouring membership system is one of their unique business points. The salon is located at station high street in Saitama. The main customer targets are the local people and the local commuters. The salon was designed and concentrated on that fitting into the local environment.

Mirrors are needed at all hair salons, and only hair stylists turn on their skills at work through freely travelling back and forth between the real world and the reflected world. The designers hope to create the space where customers can recognise their changing to beautiful in the mirror by utilising characteristic of mirror. The mirror reflects two surfaces all the time by setting all furniture away from the mirror and angled forty-five degrees.

By those devices, customer can see two different images, direct and reflected, whose figure is same but in different atmospheres. In addition, gradationally coloured floor and ceiling can connect the real world and the reflected world. In our ordinal life, the mirror exists naturally, and we never pay attention. However, there are two worlds in front of us.

1. It is a long and narrow space
2. The ceiling was designed with forty-five-degree angle
3. The storefront at night
4. The shampoo area is dimly lighted
5. Mirrors make a atmosphere be combined with reality and illusion
6. The space is simple but fashionable

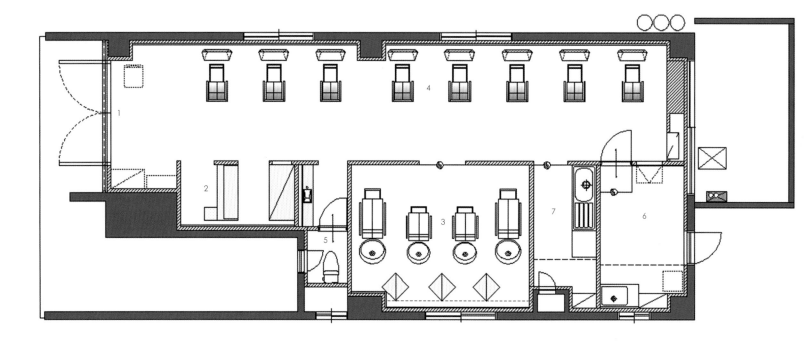

1. Entrance
2. Reception
3. Shampoo room
4. Cutting area
5. Toilet
6. Staff room
7. Lab

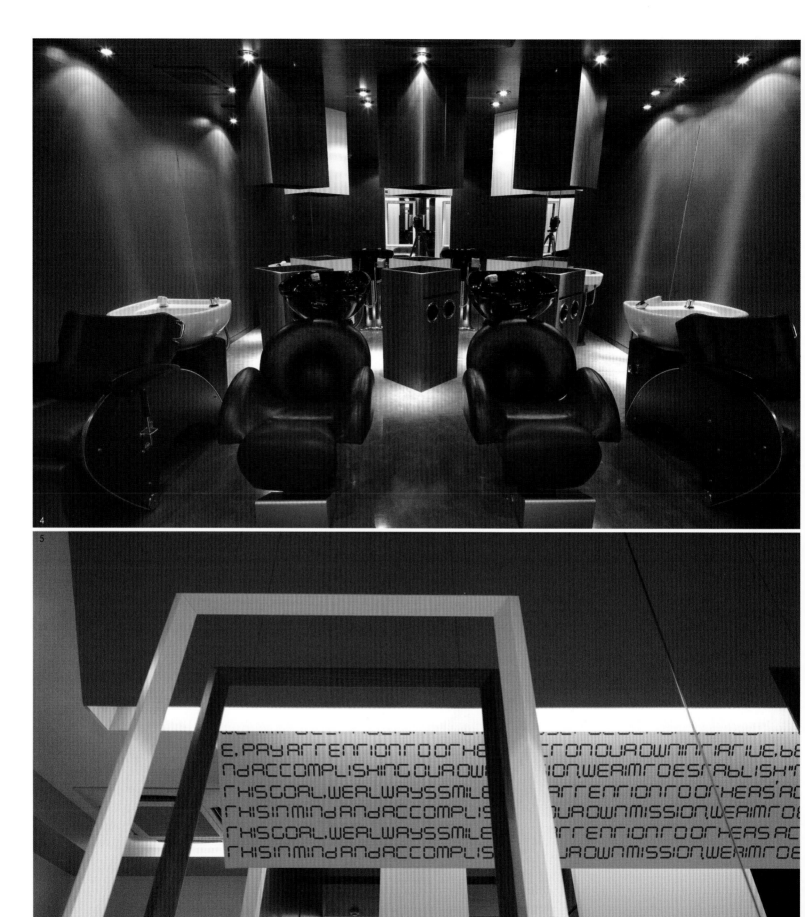

Suave Hair

Location:
Ibaraki Japan

Designer:
Kayo Hayakawa

Photographer:
Nacasa & Partners Inc.

Completion date:
2006

This building has a sharp geometric polyhedron by special shape of the site to be a symbol of this region. It makes this building characteristic.

Customers can see the beautiful scenery of plentiful trees avoiding pedestrians' eyes or people's look who is driving a car by lifting the floor 1.5 metres up from land level. While the dynamic shape, the furniture are lined up systematically, and the difference makes the atmosphere soft. To get free opening of the façade, the designers made the slanting pillar line up unequally as quake-proof wall. Because of the long span beams, there is no pillar and no partition inside to make the space flexible to use. There are several different levels inside which is made the best use of the shape, so customers can feel a wider space.

This structure which has rational function of bringing strength express both the character of symbol of the town by the outside and the inside space which is softly connected with the scenery of trees.

1. This building has a sharp geometric polyhedron
2. There are several different levels inside, so customers can feel a wider space
3. Customers can see the beautiful scenery of plentiful trees through the windows
4. There is no pillar and no partition inside to make the space flexible to use
5. The chair is simple-designed
6. The slanting pillar is a design feature
7. General view of the salon

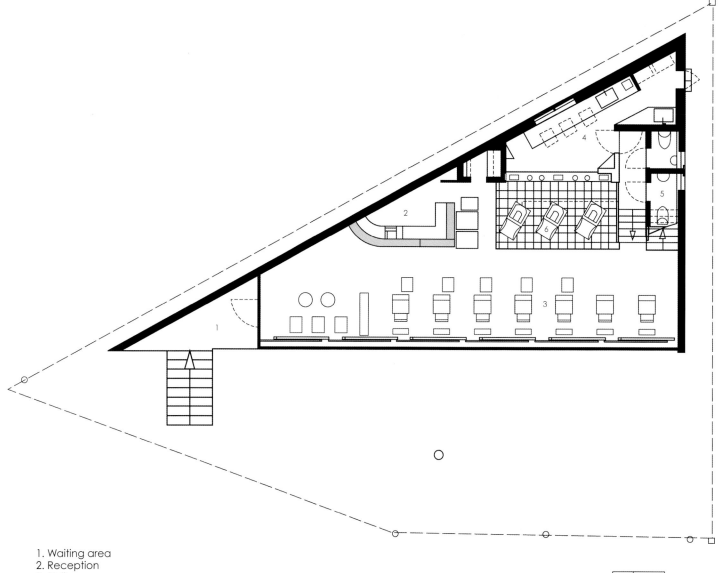

1. Waiting area
2. Reception
3. Styling area
4. Staff room
5. Toilet
6. Shampoo area

Philippe Venoux

Location:
Barcelona Spain

Designer:
Francesc Rifé

Completion date:
2008

Located on the ground floor of a former rehabilitated building in the heart of the high zone of Barcelona, Philippe Venoux has renewed its emblematic hair dressing salon, obtaining a modern and sober image. It's a space of approximately 85 square metres distributed in two areas – reception and zone of work – on a plant with irregular structure.

There's a great glazed façade that integrates the main entrance, creating a completely permeable space of transition between the exterior and the interior. The lighting is originated from the ground, accentuating the columns that distribute the space in three big openings and that allow a total vision of the space from the street: on the right, the reception, showcase and integrated built-in cupboards, and on the left, a great hanging of mirror that integrates the labelling of Philippe Venoux. Thanks to this hanging of mirror, there has been obtained an effect of geometric-cubic symmetry, saving the difficulties of the triangular structure of the plant.

The main colour of the space is white, in contraposition to the dark tone of the hair. Different elements and volumes in the project follow the same language: pavement of resins in white colour with sheen finished, specific furniture in black. This game of contrasts is presented in different areas to provide the client an intimate atmosphere.

1. View from the entrance
2. There's a great glazed façade at the main entrance
3. The exit of the staircase is surrounded by poles
4. White floor and walls contrast with black furniture

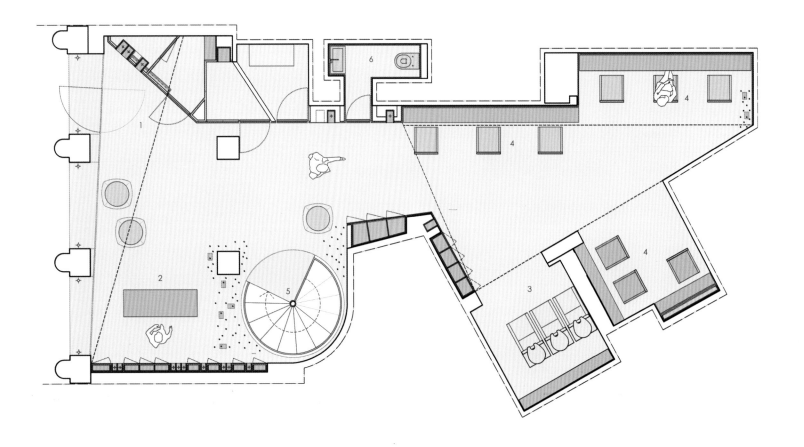

1. Entrance
2. Reception
3. Shampoo area
4. Cutting area
5. Staircase
6. Toilet

1

Arrojo Cutler Salon

Location:
New York USA

Designer:
Messana O'Rorke Architects

Photographer:
Elizabeth Felicella

Completion date:
2006

The programme for the salon was extremely simple; the designers were to provide optimum capacity for the three basic functions of the salon: hair cutting, hair colouring and product retail, and also the possibility of utilising some of the space for teaching seminars.

The form of the gutted space and the two functional elements of the programme, hair cutting and colouring, generated the design for the project. These elemental functional areas were interconnected and linked together by an axial wall. The entrance and the Aveda retail area all occur at the con joinment of these two spaces and straddle a change in level.

Long horizontal backlit stainless steel shelves, for retail products are the only elements that inhabit the monolithic brown coloured wall. Clients pass through this wall to access dressing rooms, hair wash sinks, toilets, etc. The fixtures further exaggerate the horizontal aspect of the design and break down into two categories of design format. The first category of fixtures inhabits the edge of the space between the interior and the external glass. These fixtures include the window display, retail shelves and the colour wall, all incorporate floor-to-ceiling

1. The salon's logo was printed on the windows
2. Metal elements were displayed everywhere in the design
3. The reception
4. The salon can be converted into a classroom

metal columns from which shelves, mirrors, panels, work surfaces and display vitrine are suspended. The second group of fixtures inhabits the open space; these are long narrow tables with billboard mirrors. These elements can be swung or rolled out of the way to create open space for demonstration seminars.

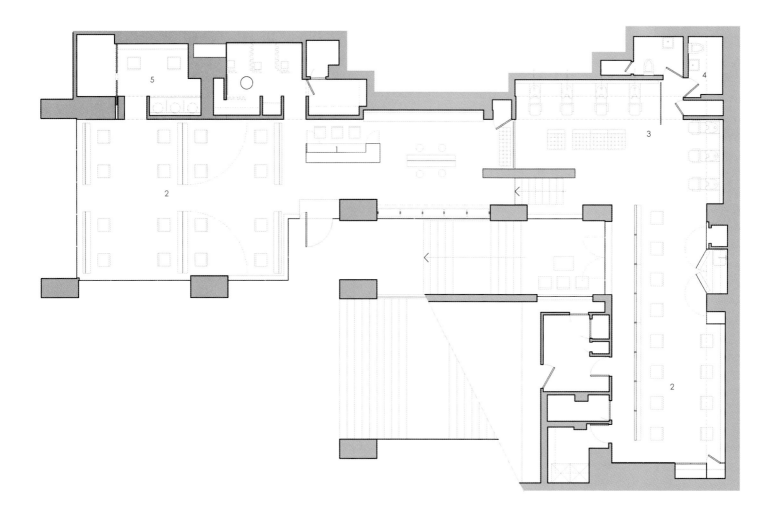

1. Reception
2. Styling area
3. Shampoo area
4. Toilet
5. Staff room

Hair salon in Kolonaki

Location:
Athens Greece

Designer:
gfra architecture

Photographer:
Fotis Traganoudakis

Completion date:
2008

The hair salon is situated in the heart of the Kolonaki area of downtown Athens. This is the area where most fashionable shops are situated. One enters the hair salon in a lower part, where one encounters the reception desk and the toilets. In the elevated level are the hairdressing and hair washing areas. Finally a more separated mezzanine houses supplementary functions such as pedicure and manicure spaces.

An atmosphere of designed contradiction was created: a clear monolithic space with a characteristic glittery plaster, encloses many elements of a decorative nature: lights, furniture, accessories etc. The shop is partly "overdesigned" to emphasise luxury, and partly left as it was found, such as the cracked terrazzo cement floor and the "bleached" wenge wooden furniture, to create less formality.

The ceiling participates by combining the functional light and ventilation with the decorative lighting fixtures, again on a background of black glitter plaster. This attitude of relaxed luxury continues in the toilets, which are cladded with gold wallpapers, protected by glass, again in combination with the existing cement floor. This environment makes the clients feel relaxed and comfortable when they are doing the hair dressing.

1. Exterior view of the salon
2. The chandelier was decorated
with feathers
3. It's a home-like space
4. General view of the salon
5. Different areas have different
lighting fixtures
6. A separate hair-dressing table

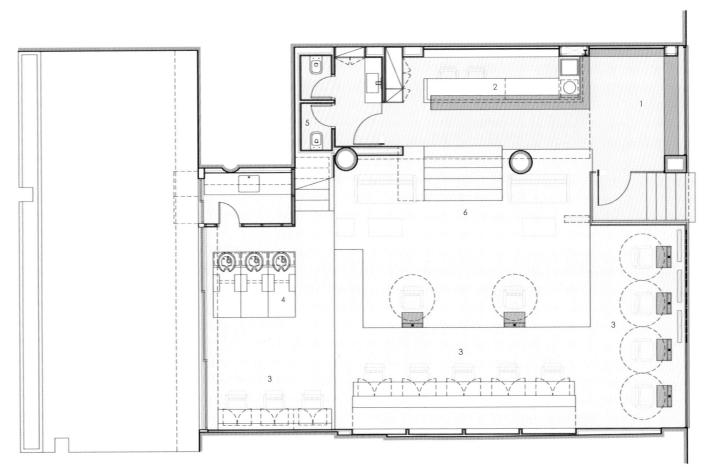

1. Entrance, window shop
2. Reception
3. Cutting area
4. Shampoo area
5. Toilet
6. Auxiliary space

Produce Hashimoto

Location:
Kanagawa Japan

Designer:
KAMITOPEN Inc./Masahiro Yoshida

Photographer:
Keisuke Miyamoto

Completion date:
2007

The "Produce" salon's concept is the customer transforms oneself. The salon transforms styles, time and feelings of the customers and renew themselves. The interior design was recreated with the concept of "transformation". Produce Hashimoto is located at a main commuting street in a private residential area, just off from Hashimoto station. The design is targeting family.

Ripples are "patterns drawn by waves on the surface of water", "influence on other people or things" and "shape that looks like a wave". Light spreads, interfering each other like ripples. As ripples cause ripples, influences infinitely grow larger and larger. Those effects create a space which goes beyond the meaning of "light". Simple action and influence, cutting hairs, infinitely spreads to customers' daily lives, life and community like stones thrown to the water.

1. Ripple patterns were repeated in the salon design
2. The warm lighting creates a comfortable effect
3. The storefront at night
4. VIP styling room
5. White furniture contrasts with black floor
6. Dark brown leather wall with grids looks luxury
7. Even the stools look like ripples
8. Shampoo area is warm and cosy

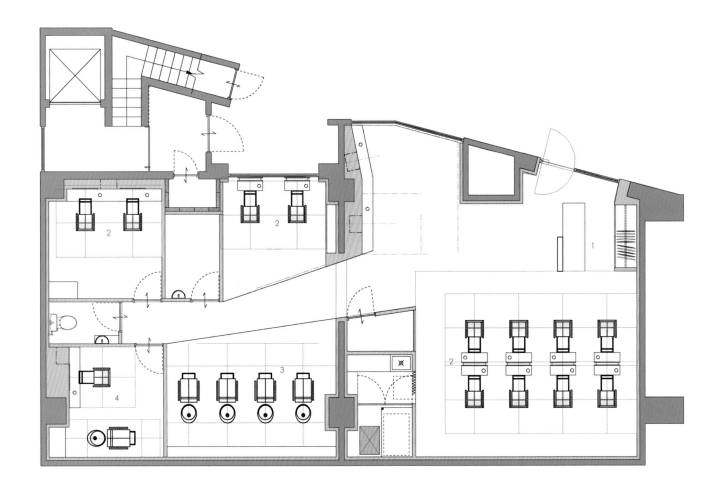

1. Reception
2. Cutting area
3. Shampoo area
4. VIP styling room

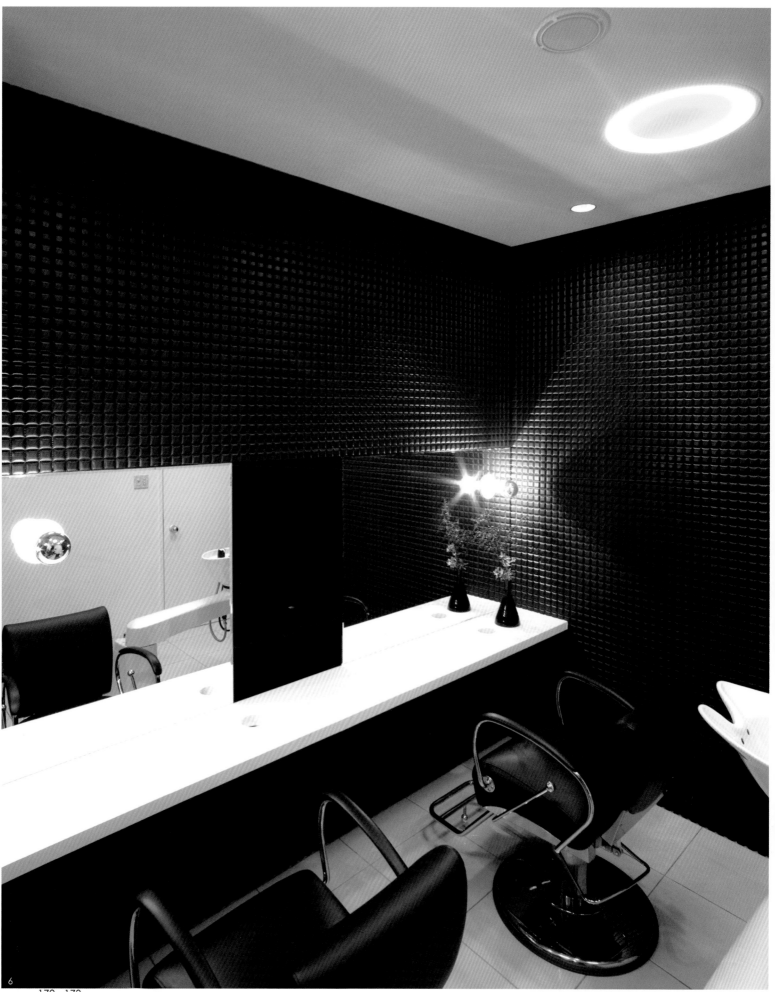

Cesare Ragazzi

Location:
Zurich Switzerland

Designer:
Rossetti + Wyss Architekten

Photographer:
Juerg Zimmermann

Completion date:
2008

The Hairdresser Cesare Ragazzi is located at Puls 5 Shopping Mall in Zurich. Six main guide walls divide the interior space in zones of various dimensions. Around the concrete core in the centre of the shop results a wide and neutral hallway, guided by the main walls. The ambiance lighting was set into the guide walls and provides the illumination of the space. The floor is the main reflector of the indirect light concept. The large sized glass boards carry natural and artificial light to the surrounding working spaces and ensure the requested privacy, although with a lack of any hermetic separation.

The overall design gives people neat lines of the structure and bright impression. The work presents a modern and elegantly simple design style. The green roof adds a pure natural feeling into the interior, but also the pure and fresh colour embrace the client. Simple and high quality feeling of the seat assembly is located in space. It makes the environment comfortable so that the clients have easy feeling.

The partitions look like crystal wall in the rain, which the texture looks quite natural and beautiful. They are not only clearly divided into the boundaries of the region, but also make room brightness, the light soft and the space comfy and cosy.

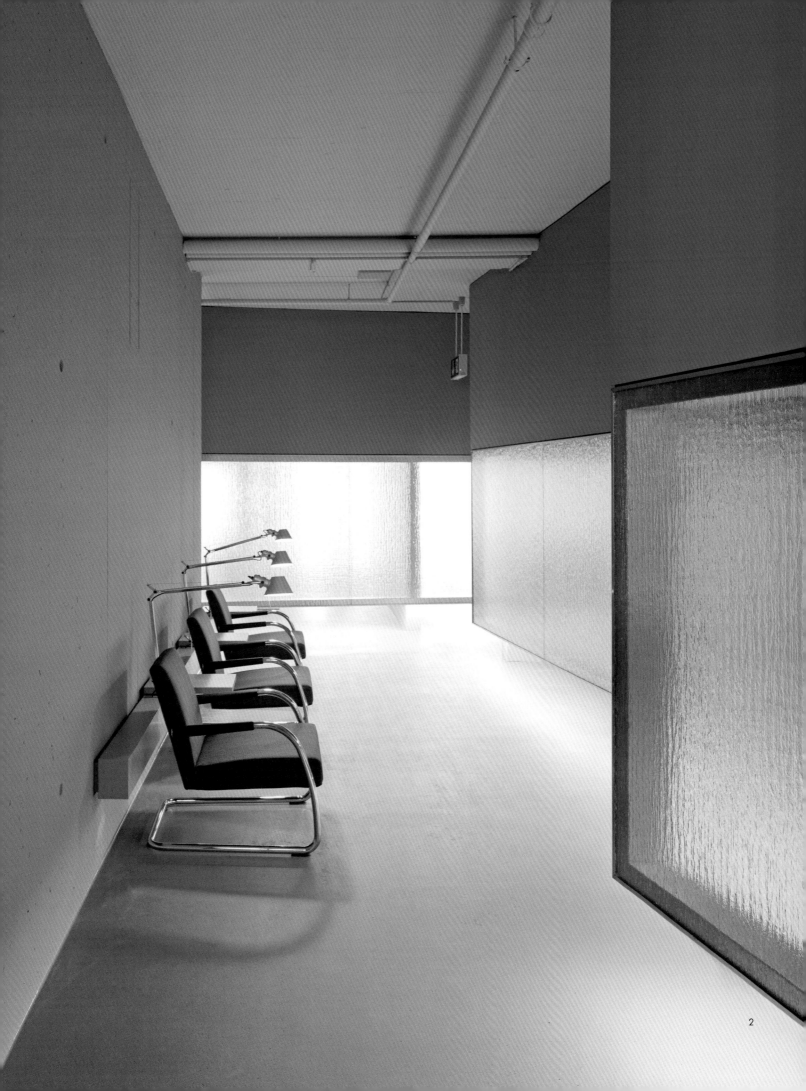

1. Simple and high quality seats are arranged in a line
2. The green roof adds a pure natural feeling into the interior
3. The partitions look like crystal wall in the rain
4. The reception
5. A hairdressing table

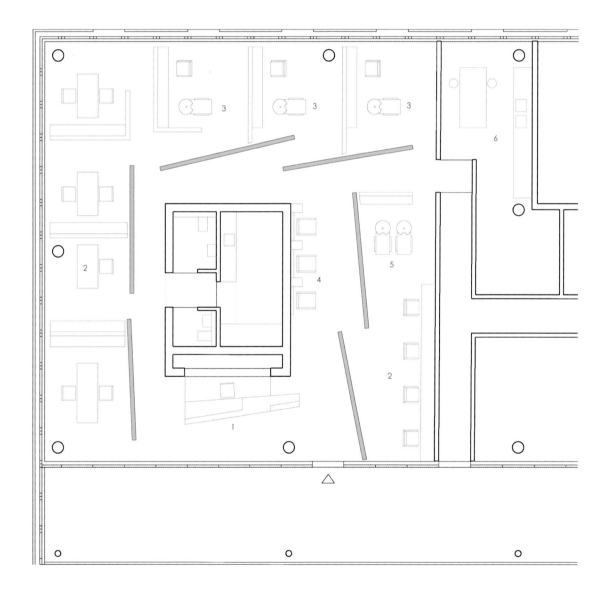

1. Reception
2. Cutting area
3. VIP room
4. Waiting area
5. Shampoo area
6. Staff room

Tan Bella Hair and Tanning Salon

Location:
San Francisco USA

Designer:
Natoma Architects Inc.

Photographer:
Rien van Rijthoven

Completion date:
2007

Tan Bella is a luxurious tanning salon located in San Francisco, California. The interior design, an elegant interior with unique wall pattern, combined perfectly with latest technology will give customers a completely different tanning experience.

Tan Bella is all covered in hairy three form panelling. The problem of cut hair falling on the floor and messing the stylish look is eliminated. The space comprises a main area with a central reception desk and cutting stations on both sides. Behind, a series of cubicles with tanning machines are arranged along a hallway. Dividing the hallway is a long and low product display table. At the end are the shampoo stations, the colouring area and restrooms.

The ambience is clubby and dark, with spotlights beaming on the patrons, and violet light radiating from the tanning cubicles along the hallway.

1. View from the entrance
2. A series of cubicles with tanning machines are arranged along the hallway
3. The reception
4. The storefront at night
5. Cutting stations
6. The walls were decorated with hairs

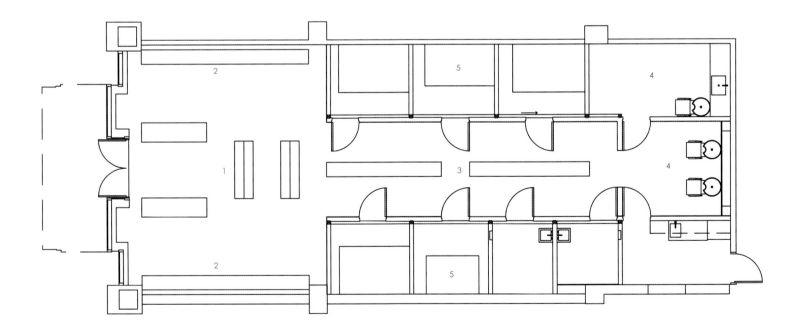

1. Reception
2. Hair salon
3. Hallway
4. Shampoo area
5. Tanning cubicles

Suite

Location:
Fukuoka Japan

Designer:
Koichi Futatsumata

Photographer:
Hiroshi Mizusaki

Completion date:
2008

This hair salon in Fukuoka City, Japan, is a "hommage to the existing tiles". Converted from an old four-storey office building, the salon is on the first to third floors, and the residence is on the fourth floor. In nowaday Japan, the opinion on the trend of "scrap and build" has just started to change. The most important subject is how to redesign old buildings and create street scenes with creativity.

The problem was how to work with the white tiled exterior which was the only character of the building and definitely not fascinating at all. Either remove all of the tiles or make good use of them. The designers tried to make a new concept using these tiles as a proof of the history of the building. The designers finally started to build the interior with other tiles and to adore these exterior white tiles. The designers used different colours and luster of tiles for the floors and the walls in the salon. The gradation of the tiles formed the character of the salon.

1. The storefront at night
2. The gradation of the tiles formed the character of the salon
3. A comfortable shampoo chair
4. General view of the salon
5. The tiles link the interior and exterior spaces
6. Wood floor adds warmth to the space

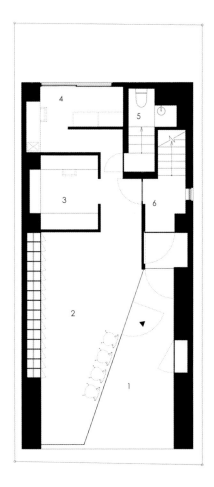
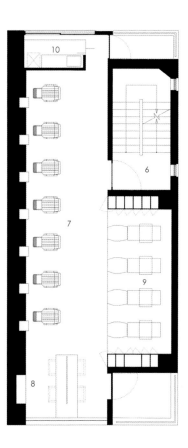
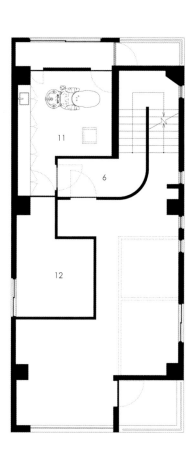

1. Entrance
2. Reception/waiting area
3. Setting area
4. Staff room
5. Toilet
6. Staircase
7. Cutting area
8. Waiting area
9. Shampoo area
10. Office
11. Head SPA room
12. Storage

Vasken Demirjian Salon

Location:
New York USA

Designer:
MSK Design Group

Photographer:
Stan Wan

Completion date:
2009

This is a highly conceptual boutique salon. The crisp white environment is a clear background, a clean palette, which accurately showcases the colour and the hair design. Sharp, clean and glossy surfaces, along with ambient soft lighting give the space a very flattering glow.

The layout in the salon is very cohesive and harmonious among the colour and styling departments which allows for effortless circulation for both staffs and customers and increases productivity. All the furniture was custom designed and built from white and red Corian, including the custom built styling "Cubes" that serve as compact and mobile storage units as well as work stations for the stylists. Dashes of red and glossy geometric shapes punctuate the interior and showcase the architecturally renowned "floating ceiling" that is composed of an intricate blanket of white cylinders that allow for a glowing diffusion of soft, ambient light perfect for hair colour.

1. The white space was decorated with colourful products
2. The floating ceiling was composed of an intricate blanket of white cylinders
3. Cutting stations and waiting area
4. There is a bar for customers to wait
5. The interior is basically in two colours: white and red
6. The shampoo area

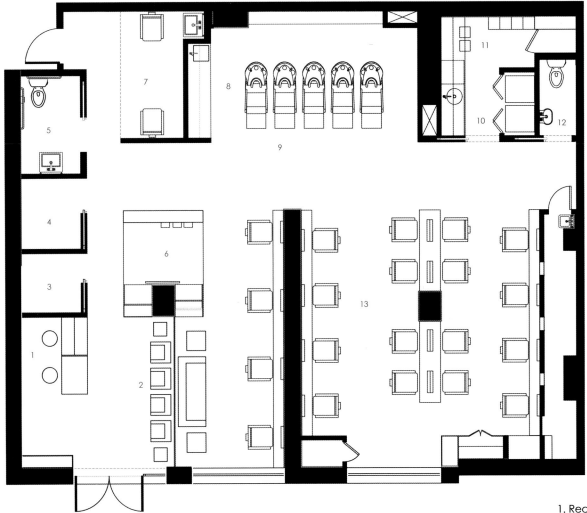

1. Reception
2. Waiting area
3. Closet
4. Changing room
5. Toilet
6. Coffee bar
7. Manicure/pedicure room
8. Colour bar
9. Shampoo area
10. Laundry
11. Kitchen
12. Toilet
13. Cutting area

1

Hairstyling Nafi

Location:
Basel Switzerland

Designer:
ZMIK in collaboration with SÜDQUAI
patente.unikate.

Photographer:
Eik Frenzel

Completion date:
2009

The most important element of Hairstyling Nafi's refurbishment is that the entrance of the salon has been wallpapered with photocopies from Vogue magazine.

The space is subdivided into two zones, which are separated by a sharp border. The two areas strongly contrast in their function as well as in their spatial atmosphere. The ceiling and the walls of the entry zone are seamlessly covered with photocopies on packaging paper made from Vogue magazines from the 1920s until today. Opulently furnished and bathed in warm light, the entry is an invitation for a rest, for purchasing products and for discussing the newest styling trends. This butts abruptly into the second segment, designed for working – it's brightly lit and bare. In the white working area nothing distracts the work of the hair stylist. The ideal light for working, the bright and glossy surfaces and the reduced furnishing put the newly cut hairstyles into the centre of attention.

1. General view of the salon
2. The space is subdivided into two zones by a sharp border
3. Opulently furnished and bathed in warm light, the entry zone makes customers feel comfortable
4. The reception

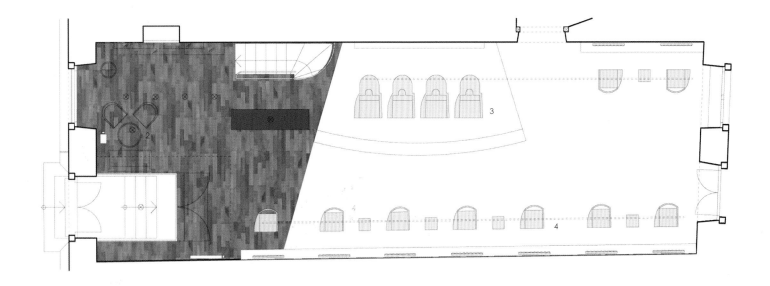

1. Reception
2. Waiting area
3. Shampoo area
4. Cutting area

Hairu Hair Treatment

Location:
Jakarta Indonesia

Designer:
Chrystalline Artchitect

Photographer:
William Sebastian

Completion date:
2009

The idea is to create a space within an existing space. The entrance is the dark colour wooden louvre on both sides. Once you enter the gate, there are six treatment areas which covered by black and white fabric to define a private treatment area for each customer. The soft material is acting as a divider that could be moved to get along with the other, and the hard material, black cotton, is acting as a permanent divider from the main corridor. The ribbon mirrors on the both side wall are carried through the view of all the space with private sight just for the client without eyes contact with the therapist. Andesit stone was applied as wall treatment. It is randomised between rough and flat side to create a distraction from a shipshape form of the design. There is continuous light above it and the mirror below is aimed to give a floating image from the floor.

Semi-outdoor experience also appears in floor finishing which is a natural texture ceramic in the waiting area and staging dark colour parquets in the treatment area that is surrounded by coral stone as the border. The only ceiling treatment is a wooden louvre with continuous lights, which acts as general lighting, along the main corridor, and the rest is black out open ceiling.

1. The space was designed along a corridor
2. The dark colour wooden louvre on the both sides of the entrance
3. The waiting area at the entrance
4. The interior lighting is soft and dim
5. Mirrors enlarge the space visually
6. The black curtain divides the individual treatment space from the main corridor

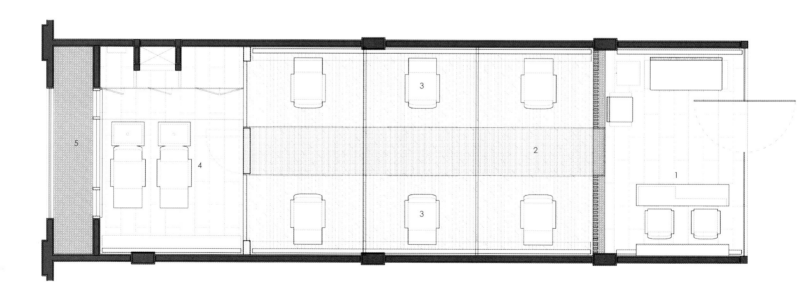

1. Reception
2. Corridor
3. Hair treatment
4. Shampoo area
5. Balcony

Sense Spa

Location:
New York USA

Designer:
MARKZEFF

Photographer:
Eric Laignel

Completion date:
2008

Sense Spa is a spa salon in Carlyle Hotel. The designers' impressive challenge with Sense was to create a space that would reflect the Art Deco style and elegance that is a trademark of the Carlyle Hotel and simultaneously combine it with the most advanced technology in the skincare and beauty industries. Faced with limited space and a landmarked New York City institution, the designers' solution was to create an incredible oasis that bridged the dramatic Busby Berkeley-esque glamour of 1940s Hollywood with clean and modern lines. This approach resulted in a jewel-like haven that is sophisticated, elegant and exudes subdued charm.

The atmosphere by design is equally glamorous and supremely relaxing. A dramatic black and gray colour scheme is highlighted with luminous lacquered wall panels, deep charcoal faux leather floors and English chandeliers. A spectacular barrel-vaulted stairwell finished in naturally shimmering platinum mosaic tiles leads to the treatment rooms. In the women's locker room as well as in the Yves Durif salon, the dark wood of the treatment rooms was contrasted with an all white design and white Carrara marble to enhance the glamour quotient. Lush patterned wool carpets and rich lacquered wood paneling and molding lend the Sense Spa a timeless, classic style.

1. Chandeliers in the reception area look like stars
2. The hair salon is a space of black and white
3. The golden staircase looks gorgeous
4. Black and white are always classical
5. In the women's locker room, white Carrara marble enhances the glamour quotient
6. Lush patterned wool carpets and rich lacquered wood panelling and molding lend the space a timeless, classic style
7. A treatment room

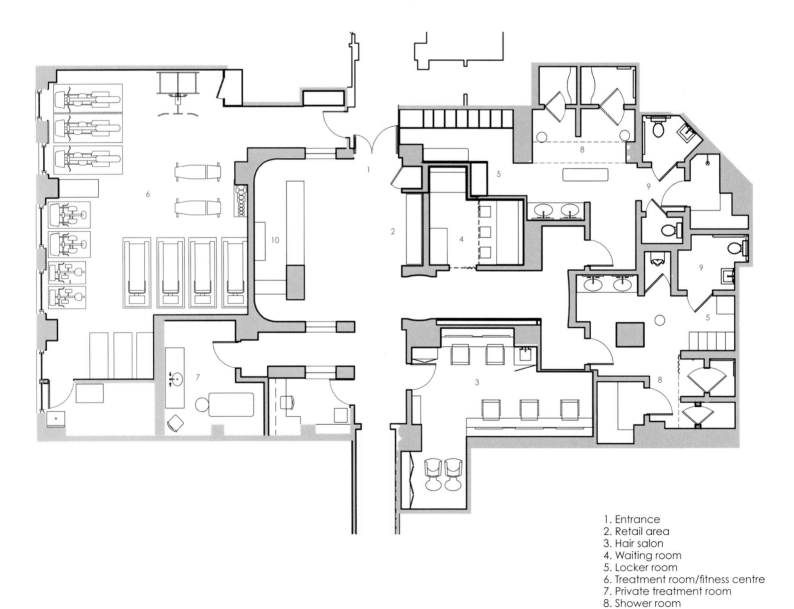

1. Entrance
2. Retail area
3. Hair salon
4. Waiting room
5. Locker room
6. Treatment room/fitness centre
7. Private treatment room
8. Shower room
9. Toilet
10. Reception

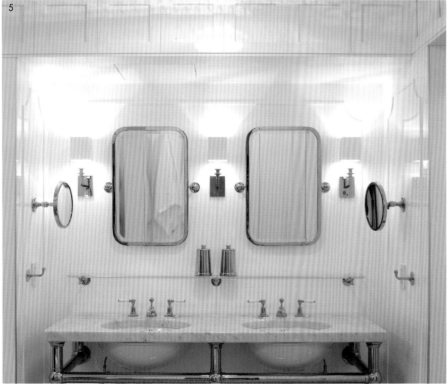

Blythe

Location:
Kyoto Japan

Designer:
YASUO IMAZU/ninkipen! Architect office

Photographer:
Hiroki Kawata

Completion date:
2008

Blythe is a Boudoir-Style salon. From shabby chic to gothic and over the top, opulent glamour is the key to this style of salon design. Black chairs and white walls, the main colours of the whole salon contrast with each other, which will supply more inspirations to the hairdressers. Customers can sit and witness the whole progress of their hair changed in such a clean and comfortable environment, making it an enjoyable experience.

When a person reflects in a large mirror, a blank increases because the area in which a person reflects doesn't change. In addition, when the mirror is inclined by five degrees and the area of ceiling in it increases, the customer can obtain a sense of freedom. Next, a shampoo space was divided from a cut space by twisting the whole. Then, two spaces should be originally optimised in sound and lighting environment.

1. Chairs of different styles make the
space Boudoir-Style
2. Customers can sit and witness the
whole progress of their hair changed
3. The whole space has a clean and
comfortable sense

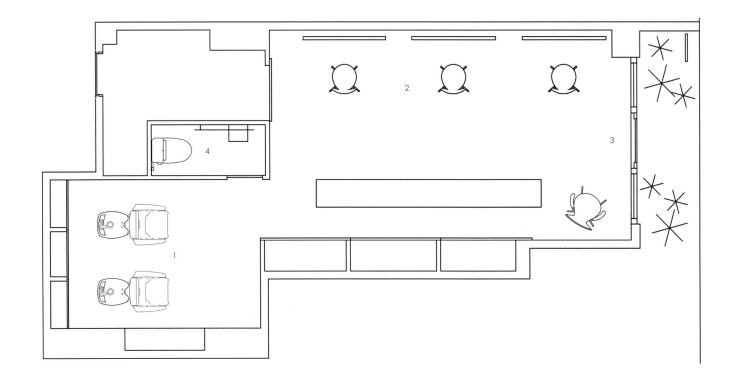

1. Shampoo area
2. Cutting area
3. Entrance
4. Toilet

Studio 1452

Location:
Santa Monica USA

Designer:
Narduli Studio

Photographer:
Art Gray, Hinerfeld Ward

Completion date:
2009

Studio 1452 – the West Coast headquarters for the KMS and Goldwell hair care brands – is a project about beauty, creation and perception. It is the launch site for a new business model that brings together three functions in one space: Hair Salon, Training Academy and Corporate Offices.

The project is located in a 1920s masonry structure within a busy retail district of Santa Monica. The designers stripped the building down to its original brick and wood truss shell. Within this industrial framework, the spaces are designed to function as discrete elements or to open up into larger interconnected zones of activity.

The street view into the building focuses on the salon. A folded white surface defines the space within the darker brick and concrete volume. This folded plane becomes reception desk, perimeter wall, colour bar, work station, retail and graphic display, storage and seating. Transparency and connection between spaces was important to the client. Glass walls and operable panels slide open to create larger rooms for events and shows.

1. The salon is an open space
2. Large screens with fashion hair styles
3. The salon has an industrial style
4. Large French windows provide
natural light for the interior

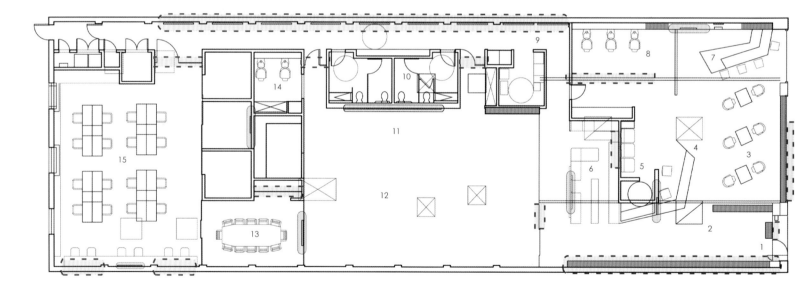

1. Entrance
2. Retail area
3. Salon
4. Reception
5. Changing room
6. Open lounge
7. Color bar
8. Shampoo area
9. Breakroom
10. Toilet
11. Modular stage
12. Academy space
13. Conference room
14. Model shampoo
15. Open office

Jenny House Beauty Salon

Location:
Seoul Korea

Designer:
Di Cesare Design

Photographer:
Zhang Yan

Completion date:
2010

Jenny House is a VIP luxury beauty salon sited in Seoul, Korea. The beauty salon is developed on two floors with an additional floor for the offices and the terrace on the roof, for private parties and special events. For the beauty salon, one floor is mostly dedicated to the wedding services – hair styling, make-up, dressing room, meeting room; the other is dedicated to the standard services – hair styling, nail design, head and foot spa. Each floor has a huge space for waiting where you can enjoy a drink while watching television or reading magazines.

The concept was based on the myth of Narcissus, the legendary guy whose beauty was acknowledged everywhere in the ancient Greece. Narcissus used to look at himself reflected on the water of the lake in the forest. Here starts the salon's story: a beautiful face built by MDF laser-cut panels. The face is reflected on the opposite black mirror, like a dark water pool in the forest. All around is the forest that the designers recreated with organic shapes that hold the mirrors. A big waving tree in the middle is functionally used as a sitting area. The white, smooth shaped metal ribbons, the reflections in the mirrors and the general atmosphere all belong to a wonderland.

1. There is a beautiful face at the entrance
2. The chairs with pearl luster look luxury
3. In the middle of the hair salon, there is a big waving tree
4. Manicure area and meeting room

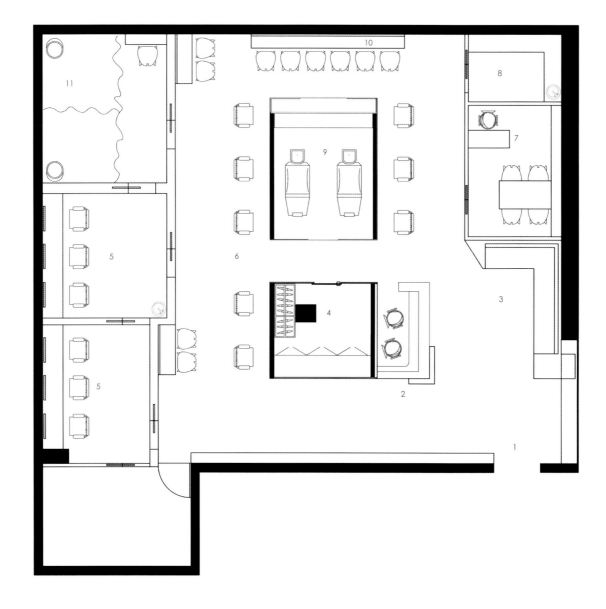

1. Entrance
2. Reception
3. Waiting area
4. Dressing room
5. Make-up room
6. Hair style room
7. Meeting room
8. Shampoo room
9. Toilet
10. Hair drying area
11. Wedding room

3

4

kilico.

Location:
Tokyo Japan

Designer:
Makoto Yamaguchi Design Inc.

Photographer:
Ken'ichi Suzuki

Completion date:
2009

Located in Daikanyama, one of Tokyo's trendiest areas, "kilico." is a hair salon housed in an attractive space in the basement of a commercial building with a skylight built in 1983 that has seen many prior tenants. The site was in an extremely stripped-down state. Even though the interior layout had basically remained the same, there were many traces left behind by previous occupants on the floor and walls – a flat mortar wall next to an unfinished concrete block wall, and a whole host of dents and depressions of various sizes in the coarse concrete floor. The designers decided to leave these textural details intact and incorporate them into the design for the new salon, so they painted the walls over in white and filled the depressions of various sizes with mortar.

Looking at the white wall that extends downwards from the ceiling until the floor, for example, you can see an entire gradient of different textures: the surface of a concrete block gradually changes into a surface riddled with holes that probably appeared when it was dismantled, which then segues into a panel with a completely flat and even finish, ending up as a fairly flat surface at the very bottom.

After the designers had filled the depressions in the floor with mortar in order to make it flat, a map-like pattern emerged that they call a "time map". The design of "kilico." is based on these vestiges of past "time" – traces of previous incarnations of this building that have been given a new lease of life.

1. The white wall that extends downwards from the ceiling until the floor
2. There are magazines for customers to read while they are waiting
3. The textural details of previous occupants are kept intact
4. There is a map-like pattern on the concrete floor
5. It is a space of pure white
6. Different areas have different lightings

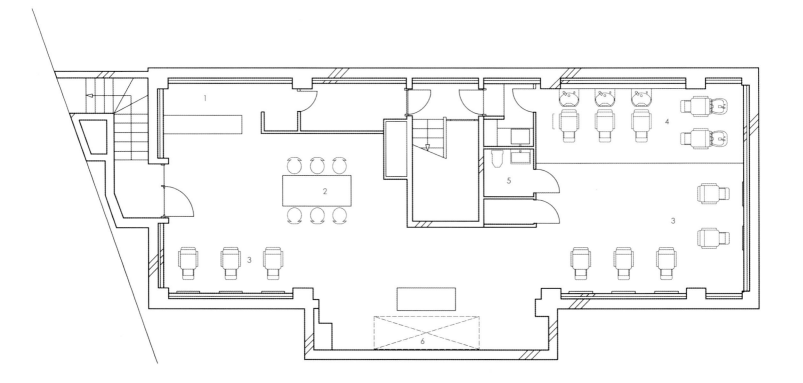

1. Reception
2. Waiting area
3. Cutting area
4. Shampoo area
5. Toilet
6. Skylight

Hair Salon at Peter Mark College

Location:
Dublin Ireland

Designer:
Garry Cohn for Douglas Wallace

Photographer:
Conor Horgan

Completion date:
2008

The hair salon studios at Peter Mark College is a creation of modern elegance. You know that you are in the height of fashion and design once you enter this high end salon. The challenge was not to overwhelm with the interior design but instead to let the space inspire new hair styling creations.

This European salon interior is clean, minimal with sophisticated architectural details throughout. The salon was also designed to have natural light enhance each studio through placement of skylight built into the ceiling of the new building addition. The open plan design predominant colours are in graceful tones white and beautiful soft greys. In contrast bright colours and patterns adorn the ceilings helping defining the different studios. All free standing styling stations are mobile and can be moved aside for fashions shows and other events that are commonly taking place on the premises.

1. The styling area
2. Bright colours and patterns adorn the ceilings
3. The colourful hair products and wall painting complement mutually
4. There is a wall painting of half scissors in staircase
5. The reception
6. The shampoo area

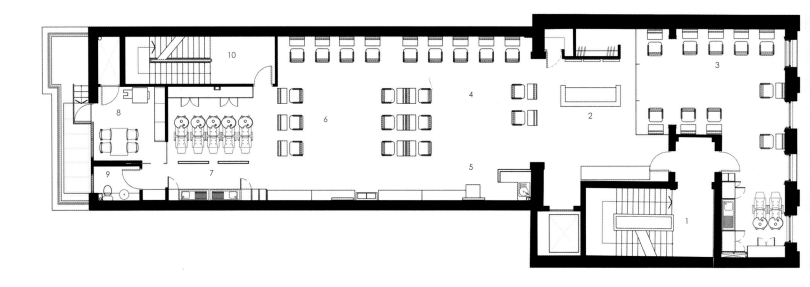

1. Entrance staircase
2. Reception
3. Senior training salon
4. Training studio a
5. Training studio b
6. Coffee bar & waiting area
7. Shampoo area
8. Teachers' room
9. Toilet
10. Fire exist staircase

5

6

1

Salon Salon Beaute

Location:
Guaynabo Puerto Rico

Designer:
Ramirez Buxeda Arquitectos

Photographer:
Robin Planas Casado
Miguel Maldonado

Completion date:
2008

The designers were instructed to maximise all work areas so as to accommodate as many clients as possible and to minimise waiting areas. Work areas for client services include spaces for ten cutting and hair preparation stations, four hair washing stations, seven hair colour stations, three manicure and pedicure stations, a massage and esthetics room, bathroom, changing room and two stations for receptionists. Other back-of-house spaces included the laboratory for the preparation of hair dyes, administrative office, laundry, storage and electrical rooms.

The materials colours and textures used on all volumes and surfaces were selected to complement the soothing, calming effect and the atmosphere of tranquility created by the lighting. A simple palette of contrasting colours and textures was used to achieve this, the cold, hard, matte surfaces of the exposed concrete fixed furniture juxtaposed against the warm tones and textures of the zebra wood veneer of the dividing boxes and against the soft cowhide and microfibre cushions. The polished, semi-reflective background provided by the grey concrete floor against the light, floating gypsum board ceiling. The translucent glass that lets light pass through, providing functions as a visual space divider and as product display background. The colours and textures also serve as visual references, the wooden boxes, the red modules, the exposed concrete benches identify the different spaces defined and created by and within them.

1. The reception and display area
2. Detail of the manicure stations
3. The hairdressing stations are slender, up to the ceiling
4. The salon has a dark colour tone
5. Detail of the precast concrete pedicure stations
6. The waiting area bench is covered with cowhide; the contrast in textures and colours is one of the main themes of the salon
7. The hair drying stations and manicure stations

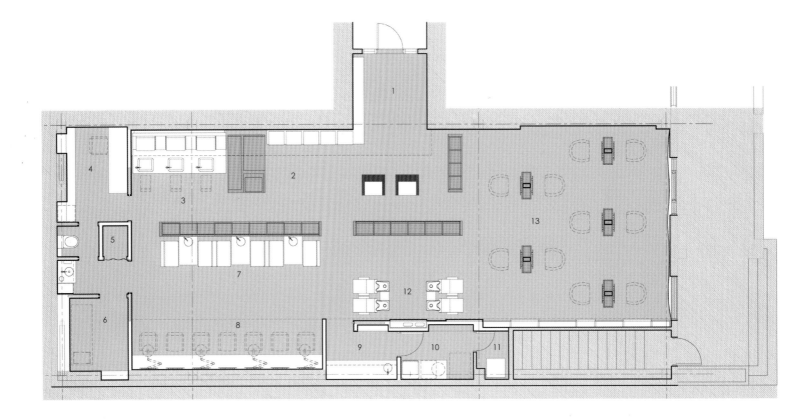

1. Entrance/lobby
2. Waiting area
3. Pedicure
4. Office
5. Change room
6. Massage room
7. Manicure
8. Colour area
9. Colour lab
10. Storage/laundry
11. Closet
12. Shampoo area
13. Cutting and styling area

Tribeca Aoyama

Location:
Tokyo Japan

Designer:
CURIOSITY Inc.

Photographer:
Nacasa & Partners

Completion date:
2006

The men's esthete salon Tribecca was designed as a place to escape from Tokyo disconnected environment and work style. The place is a gallery of mirrors and deep black walls; the precise layout of the interior creates a visual effect so when you are sitting the reflection and reality can be confusing: people entering the shop suddenly disappear from the mirror; it was only an illusion: they reappear later; the mind becomes confused.

With strong graphical elements, wood wall panels that extend on the floor are reflected by the mirrors, and create a rhythm and define the location for the customers sitting. The original leather chairs designed with angles give a visual twist within the linear interior. The shampoo area is in totally black, and the ceiling has only one light that is used to check the colours of the hairs during colourations (otherwise nothing is visible) and you can enjoy the pleasure of massage and shampoo that always take very long time in Japan. It is all about the experience, which is part of the service provided to customers, and a hair salon in this case is also a unique sensorial experience.

1. The storefront at night
2. The place is a gallery of mirrors and deep black walls
3. Wood and black contrast each other
4. The reception
5. The shampoo area is in totally black
6. The interior design elements have hard lines, expressing a masculine feeling

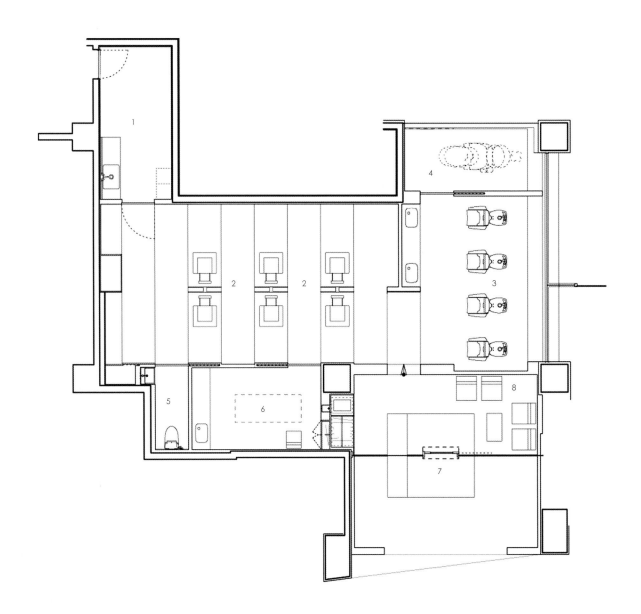

1. Office
2. Cutting area
3. Shampoo area
4. Head SPA room
5. Toilet
6. Beauty room
7. Entrance hall
8. Waiting area

Showhair Salon

Location:
Shanghai China

Designer:
Song Weijian, Guo Chun/V Jian
Design Office

Photographer:
Song Weijian

Completion date:
2009

The salon is located in a 100-year-old Spain-style building, in West Nanjing Road, Shanghai. The designers wished to keep the historical footprints in the interior design. In order to realise this idea, the designers kept the integrity of the inner structure and only made changes in the plan for functional needs. The designers used two kinds of materials: one is modern and fashionable; the other is traditional and elegant. The aim is to launch a strong contrast between modern fashion and historical footprints.

The use of a large amount of PMMC is one of the main design highlights. Windows, cabinets, lampshades, curtain boxes were all made of twelve-millimetre-thickness PMMC, so the old structures and frames were exposed well. Besides, as a fashion texture, matching up with appropriate lighting, the whole atmosphere resembles the feel of a beauty, whose both brilliant in appearance and elegant in itself.

As a VIP private hair salon, mirrors also play an important role in the whole design. The designers got inspiration from the bronze mirrors, a kind of polished bronze that ancient Chinese ladies used for making up and dressing. In order to soften the harshness in the space, the designers also applied some fur in the design, making the female customers more comfortable and showing dignity and grace.

1. General view of the salon
2. The designers got inspiration from the bronze mirrors that ancient Chinese ladies used
3. Fur elements make the female customers more comfortable and show dignity and grace
4. The reception
5. Even the washing room expresses a luxurious European style

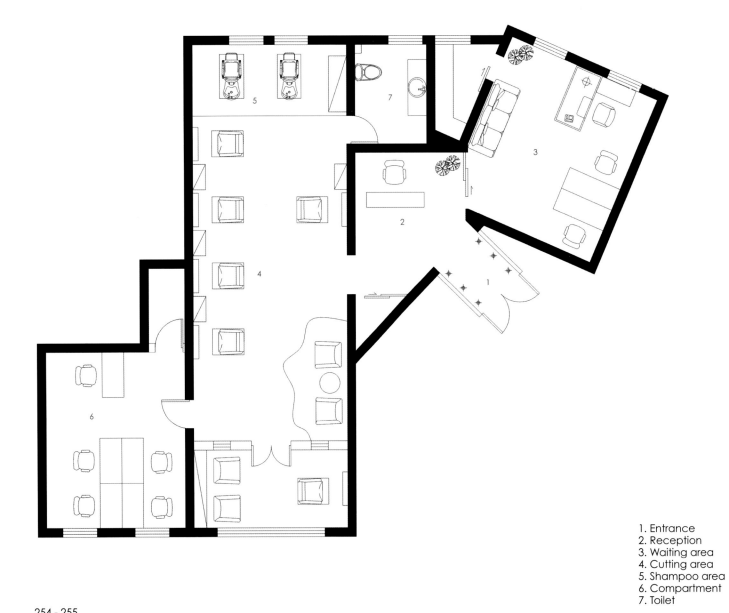

1. Entrance
2. Reception
3. Waiting area
4. Cutting area
5. Shampoo area
6. Compartment
7. Toilet

Cure Salon Monsieur

Location:
Tokyo Japan

Designer:
upsetters architects

Photographer:
Yusuke Wakabayashi

Completion date:
2009

A complex site of a beauty salon and a café, has a narrow frontage. The site is a little way off the main shopping street and on a lane. In addition, it is narrow and deep, which the Japanese call "unagino-nedoko", meaning "a bed for an eel". The client desired it to be a space for retreating. So the designers focused on utilising the depth of the site that sandwiched between two buildings and creating an interior space in which people can feel light. Thus they divided the building into three parts and slightly shifted them each other. Additionally, the designers used different materials for each part and alternate their roof pitches so that people can feel it extending far back. Furthermore, the designers put its entrance on the side and people just feel what is happening inside. This should make people want to peep into the room.

The space for hair dressing is located in the middle and has the other two parts of exterior walls as its interior wall. Moreover, it is facing the small garden and the customers will see it over the mirrors. Consequently, they can enjoy being hair-dressed inside the building just like outdoors.

1. Hairdressing tables are facing the windows, so customers can enjoy the outdoor view
2. The spatial design is clean and simple
3. The wood furniture has a low-profile luxury
4. The shampoo area
5. The salon has a masculine colour tone
6. General view of the salon from the reception

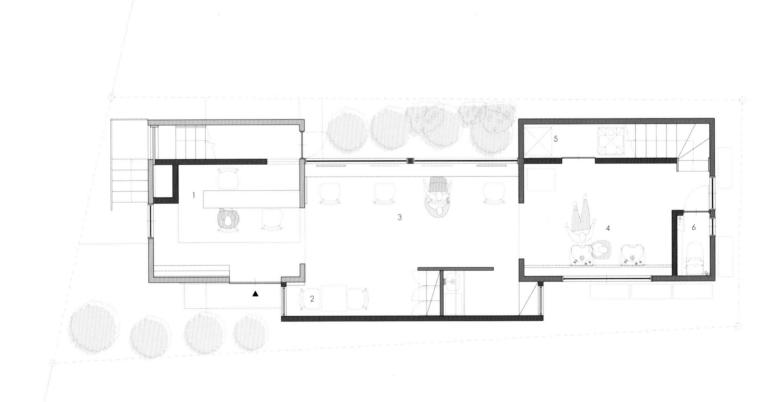

1. Reception
2. Nail corner
3. Cutting area
4. Shampoo area
5. Staff room
6. Toilet

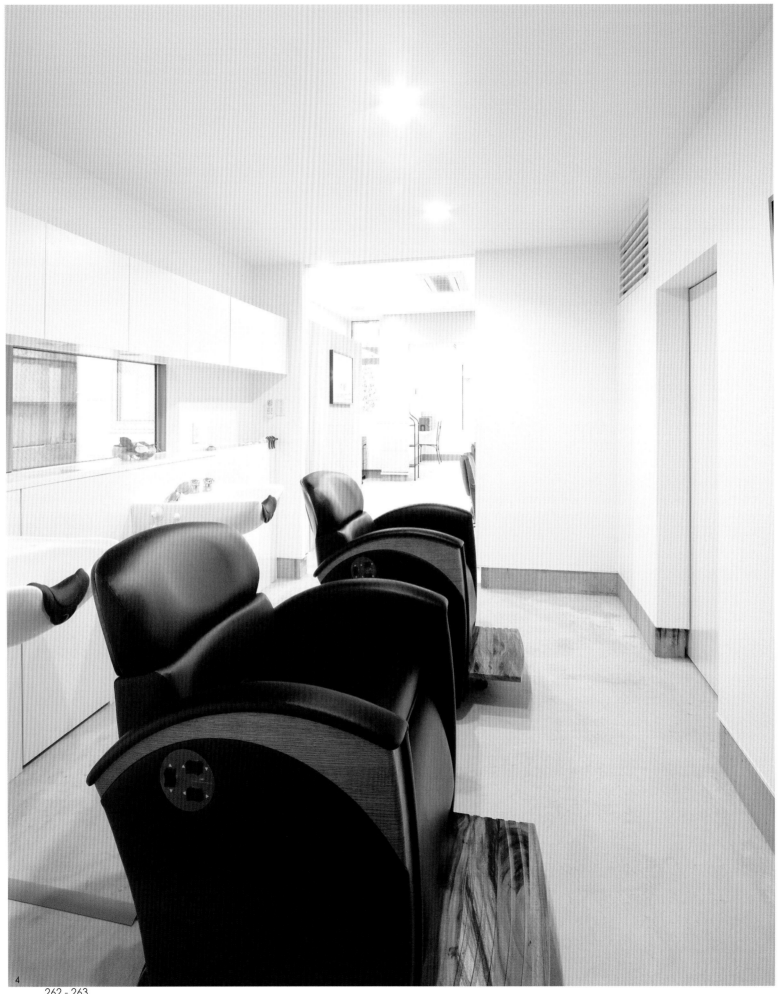

Style Club

Location:
Dublin Ireland

Designer:
Garry Cohn for Douglas Wallace

Photographer:
Conor Horgan

Completion date:
2008

The design is not minimal. Less is not more in this space – more is more and fun at the same time. Entering the traditional building you know that there is something special going on before you set foot into the space. From the street you see a wild linticular (3-dimensional graphics) ceiling in a crazy pattern with vibrant salmon coloured walls and bright white traditional moldings.

Entering the salon feels like falling into Alice in Wonderland. The design is clever with its wall of convex mirrors against a stripe patterned wall that sits next to, yes, a tartan wall – next to blue stylised clouds. This is all off set by a pink giraffe-skin printed ceiling and completed with pink giraffe-skin marshmallow shapes.

The styling stations in the middle of the room are wonderful with their candy colours and chunky geometric shapes. The shampoo area is fun. Set towards the back of the salon it was completed with five pedestals adorned with five random gold objects: a coffee cup, a baby, crayons, roller skates and a 1970s instamatic camera. And if that's not enough you will get a black and white polka dotted

1. The reception area has retained classical details
2. Entering the salon feels like falling into Alice in Wonderland
3. The shampoo area is complete with five pedestals adorned with five random gold objects
4. Bright colours fulfill the space
5. The styling stations look like Lego bricks
6. There is a "cow" in the restroom

ceiling to focus on while your hair is being treated. The reception area has retained classical details but these are contradicted by a white shiny tufted ceiling of buttoned fabric panels, with a red modern glass chandelier. There is a coffee bar that looks like it was in a time capsule that came right out of the 1980s. Furthermore there is a luxurious over-sized red velvet sofa with a large round painting of three ladies with "big hair" above. It's mad and it really works. There is nothing boring going on here.

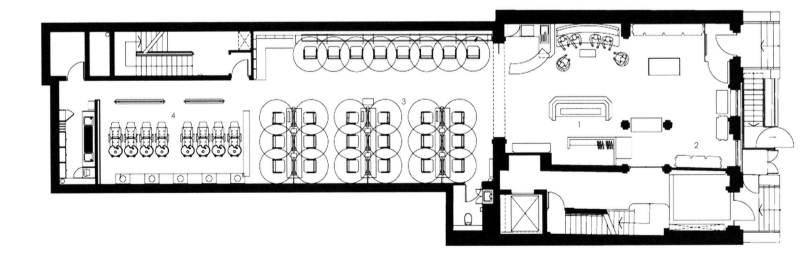

1. Reception
2. Retail area
3. Salon
4. Shampoo area

Index

Avi Oster Studio
www.avioster.com
Cristiano Cora Salon 64

BWM Architekten und Partner
www.bwm.at
Bundy Bundy 8

Chrystalline Artchitect
Hairu Hair Treatment 204

CJ STUDIO
Hair Culture 42

Concrete Architectural Associates
Bergman Beauty Clinics MediSpa 82

CURIOSITY Inc.
AVEDA Hair Salon 20
Tribeca Aoyama 246

Di Cesare Design
Jenny House Beauty Salon 224

Diego & Pedro Serrano (innova::designers studio)
www.innovadesigners.com
Carmen Font Madrid Hairdresser's 70

Edward Suzuki
Imai Colore 106

Francesc Rifé
Philippe Venoux 150

Garry Cohn for Douglas Wallace
Hair Salon at Peter Mark College 234

Garry Cohn for Douglas Wallace
Style Club 264

gfra architecture
Hair Salon in Golden Hall 130
Hair Salon in Kolonaki 160

GRAFT
Erics Paris Salon – Beijing Kerry Centre 32

Hackenbroich Architekten
Haarwerk 94

Hiroyuki Miyake
Granny. M 14

ICHIRO NISHIWAKI
Han Salon de Visage 54

KAMITOPEN Inc./Masahiro Yoshida
Tiara 88
Produce NARUSE 100
C-Style 138
Produce Hashimoto 166

Kayo Hayakawa
Suave Hair 144

Koichi Futatsumata
Suite 186

M. Design/Stephen Kuo
4 Zoom Salon 112

Makoto Yamaguchi Design Inc.
kilico. 228

MARKZEFF
Sense Spa 210

Messana O'Rorke Architects
Arrojo Cutler Salon 156

MSK Design Group
Vasken Demirjian Salon 192

Nagehan Acimuz
Scissor Hands 76

Narduli Studio
Studio 1452 220

no.555 – Tsuchida Takuya
Hair Salon Kasbah 118

Ramirez Buxeda Arquitectos
Salon Salon Beaute 240

Randy Brown
Salon Gallerie 26

Rossetti + Wyss Architekten
Cesare Ragazzi 174

Ryo Matsui Architects
Tierra 122

Song Weijian, Guo Chun/VJian Design Office
Showhair Salon 252

Stanley Saitowitz | Natoma Architect
Tan Bella Hair and Tanning Salon 180

Studio Nine
Colour Bar Hairdressers 38

Tony Kerby and John Carrabin
West Hertfordshire Hair Academy 60

upsetters architects
Cure Salon Monsieur 258

YASUO IMAZU/ninkipen! Architect office
Blythe 216

Z-A and Cheng+Snyder
La Guardia Salon 48

ZMIK in collaboration with SÜDQUAI patente.unikate.
Hairstyling Nafi 198